'Rob provides all entrepreneurs with an inspirational example of courage and determination – his life story is compulsive and compulsory reading.'

Sir John Timpson CBE, Chairman, Timpson

'Rob Law's life is an inspirational lesson in humility and resilience.'

Richard Reed CBE, Co-Founder Innocent Drinks

'A poignant memoir filled with physical bravery, entrepreneurial focus and a designers determination.'

Andrew Lynch, Associate Business Editor, The Sunday Times

'A stunningly honest and personal book from a man who has looked inside himself to make sense of the world, of business and what drives us to achieve. It speaks directly to purpose and how vital that is in business and life.'

Paul Lindley OBE, Founder, Ella's Kitchen

'Rob Law is an inspiration to us all. Read this book and you will understand why and how he's built a globally successful business and how he strives to ensure that each day counts. We can all learn something from reading these powerful pages; lessons to apply in our business, and in our life.'

Emma Jones MBE, Founder, Enterprise Nation

'Rob doesn't have the words "no" and "can't" in his dictionary. In this powerful, moving book, he shares his incredible personal story with lessons for us all about resilience and self-belief. For anyone who's got a dream, this is essential reading – but I warn you now, your excuses for not taking action will ring hollow.'

Nadine Dereza, Journalist, Presenter & Media Director

'Rob's account of his life with CF is heart-warming and deeply moving. His grit and tenacity are an inspiration.'

David Ramsden, Chief Executive Cystic Fibrosis Trust

"A truly extraordinary and inspiring story, a must read for all aspiring entrepreneurs. Rob shows how persistence, belief and hard work are the "must have" tools required to build a successful business and brand"

Richard Joseph, Co founder & CEO Joseph Joseph

"A wonderful book. . .Rob's frankness talking about cystic fibrosis and what he's doing to make lives better is inspiring"

Will King, founder, King of Shaves

"An inspirational story of resilience, hardship and humanity. I was hooked from page 1 and could not put it down. Truly anything in this world is possible."

Tom Pellereau, Inventor and Winner BBC Apprentice.

"Rob is at heart a designer, one who brings empathy, curiosity, courage and a deep optimism to overcome every hurdle and aspire to make the world better. A life affirming book for all."

Clive Grinyer, Head of Service Design, Royal College of Art

"At a time when the world is changing through a global pandemic, 65 Roses and a Trunki seems even more poignant to how we live, who we are and what we value. Rob Law's inspiring and powerfully moving story grabs you from the very first page. It's a powerful, honest and heartfelt story of survival against the odds. This is a book that everyone should read."

Professor Steven West CBE DL, Vice-Chancellor President and CEO, University of the West of England

65 ROSES AND A TRUNKI

65 ROSES AND A TRUNKI

DEFYING THE ODDS IN LIFE AND BUSINESS

ROB LAW MBE

WITH DR. PETER HUGHES

WILEY

This edition first published 2020
© 2020 Rob Law.

Registered office
John Wiley & Sons Ltd, The Atrium, Southern Gate, Chichester, West Sussex, PO19 8SQ,
United Kingdom

For details of our global editorial offices, for customer services and for information about how
to apply for permission to reuse the copyright material in this book please see our website at
www.wiley.com.

Wiley publishes in a variety of print and electronic formats and by print-on-demand. Some
material included with standard print versions of this book may not be included in e-books or in
print-on-demand. If this book refers to media such as a CD or DVD that is not included in the
version you purchased, you may download this material at http://booksupport.wiley.com. For
more information about Wiley products, visit www.wiley.com.

Library of Congress Cataloging-in-Publication Data

Names: Law, Rob, 1977- author.
Title: 65 roses and a Trunki : defying the odds in life and business / Rob
    Law
Other titles: Sixty five roses and a Trunki
Description: Chichester, West Sussex, United Kingdom : John Wiley & Sons,
    2020. | Includes index.
Identifiers: LCCN 2020000665 (print) | LCCN 2020000666 (ebook) | ISBN
    9781119628590 (hardback) | ISBN 9781119628637 (adobe pdf) | ISBN
    9781119628613 (epub)
Subjects: LCSH: Law, Rob, 1977- | Businessmen—Great Britain—Biography. |
    Luggage industry—Great Britain. | New business enterprises—Great
    Britain. | Success in business—Great Britain.
Classification: LCC HC252.5.L39 A3 2020 (print) | LCC HC252.5.L39 (ebook)
    | DDC 338.7/68551092 [B]—dc23
LC record available at https://lccn.loc.gov/2020000665
LC ebook record available at https://lccn.loc.gov/2020000666

A catalogue record for this book is available from the British Library.

Cover Design and Images: Rob Law & Phil Dobinson

Set in 10.5/14.5pt ITCFranklinGothicStd-Book by SPi Global, Chennai
Printed and bound by CPI Group (UK) Ltd, Croydon, CR0 4YY

10 9 8 7 6 5 4 3 2 1

For Kate, your bravery still inspires me today

CONTENTS

65 Roses

I n 1965, Mary Weiss volunteered to work for the Cystic Fibrosis Trust after learning that her three children suffered from the disease. Cystic fibrosis (CF) is a chronic illness that affects the respiratory, digestive and reproductive systems. It clogs the lungs with thick, sticky mucus and impairs the functioning of the pancreas. The result is a life of relentless physiotherapy, nebulisers, antibiotics and hospital admissions of varying severity. While treatments are improving and evolving, it kills most sufferers in their youth or in their prime.

When Richard was diagnosed, Mary Weiss moved the family from Montreal to Palm Beach in Florida on the advice of her doctor, who had told Mary that her children would be likely to die before they were 10 years old and the sea air would give them a better quality of life in what little time they had left.

One day, Mary's four-year-old son Richard said to her:

– I know who you're working for.

Mary was horrified. At the time, Richard confessed his knowledge of his mother's work, her eldest child, Arthur, was seven and the youngest, Anthony, was 16 months old, so she had not told any of them they suffered from cystic fibrosis or that they would be likely to die young. Her relentless phone calls aimed at raising money for the Trust were often done from home and now, confronted by her son, she feared the worst. He must have heard her use the words 'cystic fibrosis' many times and perhaps he had learned what it was and that he had it.

– What am I working for, sweetheart? she asked, nervously.

– You're working for 65 roses.

Mary burst into tears when she realised that when she said cystic fibrosis, her son heard 65 roses.

Time treated the family harshly. Arthur, the eldest child, died young and Richard also lost his battle with cystic fibrosis, while Mary continued to battle for a cure until her death at the age of 77 in April 2016.

One of Mary's many legacies is that children who suffer from CF still refer to the illness as 65 roses. As a sufferer myself, I'm touched by this story of how an ugly genetic illness came to be associated with the scented beauty of roses.

This ambiguity defines for me the delicate balance between life and death, success and failure. As with all such stories, luck plays a pivotal role. To get CF, both parents have to be carriers of the relevant genetic mutations, which means the odds of the disease being passed to me were 25%. As an entrepreneur, the odds of me creating a global brand and becoming a millionaire were vanishingly small. Yet, when the dice rolled, I got the illness and the global brand.

Would I prefer the dice to have behaved as the odds predicted, making my health good and my bank balance empty? I never ask myself questions like that. We get the life we are given and all we can do is make the most of it, and that is what makes writing this book such a difficult task. Is it a book about battling terminal illness? Or is it a book about a product I designed while at university that changed the way children travel? Or is it perhaps about what it takes to start with nothing, be ridiculed by experts and go on to prove everyone wrong?

In fact, it is a book about all these things. Regardless of whether we are born with a genetic disorder that is likely to kill us in our youth, we will all, at some point in our lives, have to fight illness and misfortune. If we start our own businesses, we will all have to fight for the cash to keep our dreams alive. Most businesses will perform modestly and many will go bust. The rich and successful entrepreneur is the exception that proves the rule.

In sickness and in health, through success and failure, the course our lives take is often random and unpredictable, but how we deal with the randomness is not. That small slither of opportunity where we can manage the unpredictability that envelops us on all sides is what we can control. Fighting for your life or making your first million requires the same skills of courage, emotional discipline and a capacity to deal with unfairness and adversity without becoming a victim of either. This book is about those skills, what they are and how you can learn them. They are tools for life and I will do my best to teach them by telling my story about what it means to defy the odds in life and business.

A Promise

L ives turn on small details.

Mine turned on a knock on a door.

A tall, thin man with a scruffy beard came into the classroom. I didn't know he was coming for me, so I carried on with my work.

I heard whispers. I looked up and saw him talking to the teacher. They glanced across at me as they spoke. There was something in their gaze. I didn't like it. It's the way people look when something breaks the familiar patterns of the world and turning away isn't an option.

The tall, thin man with the scruffy beard walked towards my desk.

Whatever he'd brought into the classroom, it was for me.

There were five boys and one girl in our group. We'd just begun our A levels and this was the first day of *An Introduction to Engineering*, a three-day course at Loughborough University. The problem we'd been given to solve was how to design a retractable platform to allow people to get closer to the wing of an airplane during production.

This was the kind of problem I liked. It had a solution. It wasn't messy.

The tall, thin man touched my shoulder.

I froze.

– Rob, he whispered, you'd better come with me.

I followed him out into the corridor. I knew what was coming. I brushed my shoulder with my hand, as if to wipe the knowledge away. It stuck. I tried again.

– It's your father. He's on the phone and he needs to talk to you.

We went into his office.

– Dad? I said.

– Rob . . .

He paused.

I knew.

Please don't talk to me. Let me go back in.

– . . . It's Kate . . . he said, his voice frail.

Please, please, don't let it be.

– . . . she's not going to make it, Rob, and you'd better come to Great Ormond Street Hospital.

Small details, like a knock on a door, change lives.

Of course, I should have seen it coming.

Like me, my twin sister had been born with cystic fibrosis. Twenty months before the knock on the door she'd had a heart and lung transplant. She'd either been doing well or, as most of us do when faced with our deepest fears, we chose to see hope. On the anniversary of her transplant the local paper ran a feature headlined: 'Brilliant new life for Kate aged 15'.

Along the top of the page ran another sentence in bold: 'Celebrations one year on after breath of fresh air'.

The article continued in the same vein with the paper quoting Mum saying that Kate 'is living a completely normal life and the beauty of the new lungs is that they won't clog up because they are not genetically hers. It was an awful life when I look back and a year later it was impossible to tell she ever lived in the shadow of death'.

A few months before the 'shadow' returned, we went to Canada for a family holiday to celebrate Kate's new future. When she got back, her body began rejecting the donated organs. Every day she got worse. She spent Christmas in Great Ormond Street. I still have the picture of her lying, asleep, on her bed, wearing a thin blue hospital gown. Behind the bed is a teddy and a balloon and cards and Kate just lying there, eyes closed, drifting away.

A man, dressed as Father Christmas, stands next to her, holding an unopened present. He's staring at the camera, an uncertain look on his face, struggling to understand how his gifts can change anything. Only a few weeks earlier, we were on holiday. Playing Gameboy. Laughing. Squabbling. We saw the Rockies and stayed in Vancouver and Edmonton. We travelled through dense forests and, if I close my eyes, I can still smell the fresh, earthy scent of pine trees that takes me back to a time when the future felt safe. I, like our family in Canada, felt blessed that Kate was doing well. She wasn't well, of course, but feelings are insistent. They pester you until they're believed and maintaining a semblance of normality is enough for us to bury what we know. We keep feeling and hoping until our emotional illusions are shattered and we're left, stranded, staring at nothing, like detectives hunting a criminal only to find every house empty. We're a sluggish species, always playing 'catch-up' with our own lives and all it takes is a knock on a door to remind us, to wake us from our slumber, to hurl us, screaming, into a world we've buried.

Kate was dying and, despite the facade of denial, I knew it. When what we fear is too real to bear, we turn away. When the knock on the door came, I convinced myself it was just a knock, like thousands of other knocks I'd heard before. Even when I heard my father's voice, breaking as he spoke, I thought everything would be alright. It had to be because it wasn't just about Kate. It was about me. I suffered from the same illness and her destiny was also mine.

Mr Blackford drove me to London in a minibus. Just the two of us. He sat in the front. I sat behind. It was dusk when we left and the January sky loomed dull and grey. We drove in silence. I was numb. Facing Kate's death meant facing my own future and I was more comfortable building things, like retractable platforms, than I was imagining my body breaking apart. So, I built a wall. An imaginary one as solid as any wall that's ever been built and I stuck my illness behind it. If any of the bricks fell away, even if there was a crack in the mortar, then what broke through might be stronger than me, so I kept this 'other life' hidden, a secret I kept from myself.

As we travelled down the motorway, I took refuge in the reassuring hum of the engine. The silence trapped me and Mr Blackford in separate worlds. It kept the wall intact.

It was late when we arrived at Great Ormond Street.

Too late.

Kate was dead.

My Dad told me she died two hours before we arrived. They'd turned her life support off. They had no choice. Whatever they did, she was going to die quickly. An act of love, turning the machine off protected her from senseless suffering.

Mum cried uncontrollably. I hated seeing her heart break. *There's worse off than you,* she said to us when we grew tired of taking our medicine or when the shadow of our illness was too dark. Now, staring at Kate, my mother slipped into a dark hole, my father more helpless than I'd ever seen him before, my brother only eight years old, his world no longer safe, and me, numb, not knowing what to do or say.

The supports of my life were falling away and all I could do was stare at my sister, lifeless, her eyes closed. I have no idea how long I stood in the room, tracing the lines of the tubes that stretched from her body to the machines around her bed. I kept expecting her to move. Smile like she used to. Do something to annoy me. Anything. Everything inside me froze and I knew if there was a thaw in my heart, I'd lie next to Kate and die with her.

At some point, I must have left the room where Kate lay because someone asked me, my mother I think, if I wanted to stay or go back and finish the course at Loughborough.

I chose to go.

Nobody asked me why or if I was sure I wanted to leave.

If they'd asked me, I wouldn't have had an answer to give. I'd lived my life as if it was normal, as if cystic fibrosis was nothing more than an inconvenience and now I was facing the truth.

I hated the illness. It was alive, as close to me as death and as distant as a star. Me and not me. Mine and not mine. My only defence was to refuse to let it consume me.

We drove back in the same minibus, the silence brutal and comforting. This time, the numbness was more complete. Push a needle through my hand, I thought, and I'll feel nothing. I can't afford to.

When we got back to the university, it was the middle of a starless night.

I felt alone, my twin sister dead, killed by the illness we shared.

I remembered the knock on the door. A quiet, apologetic knock that tore my life in two. Such misery often comes from events that force their way into our lives with the fury of sudden storms. Yet these storms mature slowly in our sightline. It's the lag before they strike that gives us the comfort of denial. So we look away until our lives are shattered. It's a familiar pattern. This is mine:

1. I was told my life would be shorter than most.
2. Despite the relentless routine of drug taking and therapy, most days I felt well enough to deny this knowledge.
3. The more I carried on as normal, the more I convinced myself I wasn't ill.
4. Then my twin sister got sick and had a heart and lung transplant and I convinced myself she'd make a full recovery.
5. Then came a knock on the door.
6. Followed by a vigil at Great Ormond Street Hospital where I arrived too late to make a difference.
7. The journey back to a university and the resumption of an engineering course, gave me the space to embrace the necessary illusion of normality.

If you think this pattern is strange, it isn't. We all do it because we must, the only difference being that you probably have the luxury of a more plausible denial than me and denial is built in just the same way as retractable platforms or children's ride-on suitcases. It begins with a compulsion to create and is sustained by a process of trial and error that never ends. It doesn't matter that nothing is ever completed to the point of perfection, not lives, not products, not businesses, nothing. The key is that you have to persist and it's this very act of persistence that creates an illusion of progress. It routinises our lives and, where there is routine, there is belief that storms will pass us by.

I remember a quote from Ernest Hemingway:

'How did you go bankrupt?' Bill asked.

'Two ways', Mike said, 'Gradually and then suddenly.'

That's how it happens. We persist in our routines, every day making the world more familiar, more solid, less likely to break. In business, we come to the same office, speak to the same people, nurture the same clients, analyse the same projections, and all the while the ground is shifting under our feet.

. . . Gradually

Then one day, we notice that this gradual shifting has taken a turn for the worse: the ground isn't there anymore and we're falling, fast.

. . . and then suddenly

People who die, like businesses that fail, don't want it to happen. We fight to keep breathing like we fight to keep cash in the bank and balance sheets solvent. Stopping breathing or going bust are demons we deny. We're good at denial because we're hopeless optimists, continually misreading the world, making it more benign, tamer, than it is. The pay-off is that we sleep at night, imagining tomorrow or, at worst, the day after tomorrow, will be better than today. The downside is we don't see the danger until it's too late. Later, when we look back at the devastation, we wonder how it was we missed the signs.

. . . Kate had cystic fibrosis.

. . . A heart and lung transplant at 15.

. . . What did I expect the outcome would be?

The answer is I expected her to live and hope was the last thing I lost.

In Greek mythology, Pandora, the first woman, is created by Zeus to punish the human race for the theft of fire from the gods. She's given a jar and when it's opened all the evils that inflict us are released into the world. When the evils escape, human life is full of suffering. However, one evil remains in the jar: *elpis*, the Greek word for hope or expectation. When I first heard the story I never understood why hope was an evil. I do now. For anyone who has seen a loved one die of cystic fibrosis or cancer or any long illness where emotions swing from hope to despair in weeks, days or even hours, living in constant expectation of recovery against all odds is both what keeps us fighting and breaks us when the battle is lost. Perhaps this ambiguity is why *elpis* stayed in Pandora's jar: hope, despite its capacity to wound, also sustains us in our darkest moments. I didn't know it at the time of Kate's death, but the degree of serenity in our lives is in direct proportion to the lowering of our expectations: if we expect immunity from suffering, we will live lives of quiet, corrosive desperation. If we expect nothing, we are likely to live a happier life, because we are less at the mercy of events outside our control.

After Kate died, I decided that most things that happen to us are unbearably random and it was easier to immerse myself in my passion for design and creativity than it was to expect anything to work itself out for the better. When I'm designing, creating, planning, I'm absorbed in the moment, without a past or a future, a pure present, free from suffering. So that's where I've lived the best parts of my life, the place where everything I've ever designed is created and where I go when I'm fearful of the illness that stalks my life.

I must have slept a few hours before going back to the classroom at Loughborough University.

At first, my classmates were that awful mixture of pity and fear, shuffling their feet, talking to me in whispers and broken sentences. I didn't want to talk about Kate. I wanted everything to be normal. They must have sensed that because, after these awful moments without any emotional geography, they got on with the day. And so did I.

I spoke to my parents in the evening. They asked how I was.

– I'm okay, I said, and the course is good.

They talked about arranging the funeral.

– I don't know when it will be yet, Mum said.

– Okay, I said.

I didn't say anything else. To myself or to them.

By the third and final day of the course, life felt normal again. I let habit and routine take me to a place where I could get on with living, a sanctuary like the emotion that kept the poet Matthew Arnold from breaking under the pressure of a lost love: 'we forget,' he wrote, 'because we must'. That's why, on the second night after my return, I went to the pub with my classmates. I don't remember much, only the name, the Frog and Firkin, the rattle of shoes on wooden floors and foam on my lips, the residue of waves I'd sunk with my beer. My forgetting was, of course, brittle. I knew I could never forget the twin sister I loved or the image of her, lifeless, in a hospital bed. But I knew I had to do my best to move on with my life or be crushed by the loss. The illusion held for as long as I was away from home. Physical separation can bring emotional distance in its wake and, when I returned to school, Kate's friends stood in the drizzle to greet me. The illusion shattered and I wept uncontrollably, unable to recover myself until I was alone.

Between death and burial there's a hiatus, a gap in the rhythm of a life that's finished and not finished at the same time. I can't remember much of what I did during that time. I remember feeling numb and, when that feeling thawed, overcome with rage at the unfairness of everything. What had Kate done to deserve this? She was kind and brave and funny and smart. And now she was dead.

Yet, my mother's grief was, if anything, more unbearable.

In this hiatus, people came to visit. Dozens of them. Every time a new face arrived at the door, the wound in Mum's heart deepened. I watched her repeat the same grief over and over again and I grew to dread a knock on the door and hate the people who came to give their condolences. They meant well and, when a person dies, especially one as young as Kate with her whole life ahead of her, it opens buried grief we all carry for the losses we've suffered and the losses we know are to come. It's often only through the suffering of others that we truly feel our own pain.

Despite this, I hated the impact on Mum. She, more than anyone, didn't deserve this. She'd taught us to feel blessed we were alive.

She made sense of our suffering and now all I could see was her pain, haemorrhaging in the direction of every visitor that came. She greeted them with what strength she had left. When the door closed behind them, she sank, exhausted and overwhelmed.

I wanted a deal with God: turn the clock back, I said, make all this pain not happen and I'll . . .

That's where I got stuck. There was nothing I could give, real or imagined, big enough to cut this deal. Paralysed by guilt at being the first born, the one who survived, I had nothing to give except my life.

Minutes, hours, days passed and the funeral got closer. Mum and Dad busied themselves with the practicalities of the funeral. It gave them a purpose, a way of loving Kate that anchored her presence, however fleetingly, in the proximity of the world.

We drove the short distance from our small hamlet to Tarvin Church, where the funeral was held. A dark, grey January day. I don't think it rained. I bore the coffin with my uncles. I remember the hollow crunch of my shoes on the gravel, music I can't name and faces pressing against me.

After the service, we buried Kate in a far corner of the graveyard. The long, slow walk from the church door to the grave felt like it would never end. It did, of course, and afterwards, Mum wrote a letter to friends and family. In the fourth paragraph she wrote, 'In August, we had the best family holiday we could have had' and, as if to prove how quickly things change and how unprepared we are, the fifth paragraph begins:

> During this holiday Kate showed signs of not being quite right . . . On our return, September and October were spent trying to find out why she was less than 100% . . . All the tests

14

carried out could find nothing wrong . . . After still no signs of a reason, from the multitude of tests carried out, her breathing started to deteriorate . . .

That's how tragedy unfolds, a slow, unfathomable descent into our deepest fears. Mum's response to this is typical: 'It is,' she wrote, 'so hard to understand why'.

The question of meaning or purpose, the 'why' question, is the hardest one to answer. In the years immediately after the Second World War, the Jewish psychiatrist Viktor Frankl was interned in Theresienstadt in 1942 before being moved to Auschwitz and finally to a labour camp. Only he and his sister, Stella, survived. Determined to make sense of his suffering and the wasted lives of his family, Frankl wrote *Man's Search for Meaning*, in which he wrote that 'those who have a "why" to live for, can bear with almost any "how"'.

More than 60 years after the publication of Frankl's book, the author Simon Sinek returned to the same themes in his groundbreaking business book, *Start with Why*, in which he wrote: 'very few people or companies can clearly articulate *why* they do *what* they do. By *why*, I mean your purpose, cause or belief – *why* does your company exist? *Why* do you get out of bed every morning? And *why* should anyone care?' He concludes that people 'don't buy *what* you do; they buy *why* you do it'.

If meaning or purpose, 'why' is the primary driver in life and business, then everything else we chase, like wealth or success or happiness, is just an effect of our ability to ground our lives and our businesses in a strong sense of purpose. 'Success, like happiness', wrote Frankl, 'cannot be pursued, it must ensue'.

In the weeks after Kate's funeral, I found it hard to find any meaning in her death. I withdrew into myself and, if there was any purpose in my life at that time, it was for Mum to stop hurting. I had more empathy for her than I did for myself. I often struggle to feel compassion for myself. Only when I'm in hospital for treatment or when the cystic fibrosis impairs the routine of my life, do I even get close to feeling for myself the love I feel for my parents, my family and for Kate.

So I went as often as I could to Kate's grave. Sometimes I spoke to her. Other times I stood in silence, not sure what to say or feel. As teenagers Kate and I were very different people. She loved books, while my dyslexia made it difficult for me to read. She excelled at school until her health declined, while I was put into the special needs class. What bound us was the illness we shared.

At junior school, we were kept together to take our medicine and to make sure we didn't eat fat. We looked with envy at other children playing outside while our daily routine was driven by managing our illness. This routine didn't just affect our school lives. It began first thing in the morning when Mum made sure we did our physiotherapy to keep our airways clear. This involved breathing in different patterns and moving the body into various positions, mostly with head tipped lower than the body. Once in this position, I'd tap on my chest like a drum to create a percussive effect which drained secretions and ventilated my lungs. We also took our drugs and nebulisers before we went to school and the routine repeated after school with more physiotherapy, nebulisers, and ended last thing at night with more drugs before bed. Dad once drilled a hole in the living room wall through which a small plastic tube passed, which meant we could nebulise our drugs without Mum, Dad, and David, my younger brother, inhaling the fumes.

Despite the many ways in which cystic fibrosis distanced me from my friends, I craved normality. Some days I didn't do my physiotherapy and went running with my father. As a teenager I began weightlifting to build body mass, which enabled me to store the energy I'd need if

I fell ill. I took up cycling. It gave me freedom and allowed me to visit friends in nearby villages. At 13, I started a paper round. Driven by an unarticulated drive to defy my illness and live a normal life, I created my own routines and found meaning in turning my illness from a dark, unmanageable shadow that hung over my life to a practical problem to be solved.

After Kate's death, Mum became committed to a kind and gentle Christian faith and threw herself into raising funds to find a cure for the illness that killed her daughter and that would, one day, kill me. That was never going to be my path to meaning. I had no religious or philosophical answers to the question of why Kate died or why I and many others live with incurable illnesses or find ourselves victims of circumstances beyond our control. Of course, it's all unfair but moaning about unfairness when you can do nothing to change what you're moaning about is a certain path to misery.

What, then could I do?

I couldn't let my life get stuck in visits to Kate's grave or in grief. I hated watching Mum collapse under the weight of grief then pull herself up only to repeat the cycle again. If there was a meaning in this suffering, I found it in an act of defiance. I had no control over the fact that Kate died. I had no control over the fact that I, too, might die from the same illness. But I did have control over what I did with my life. Whether I chose to be crushed under the weight of what I was carrying or whether I chose to live my life well.

I chose to live.

I made a promise to myself. I promised that Mum would never grieve over me. Kate was the last child she would lose. Determined to defy my prognosis, I took control over my life in the best way I knew, which was to solve the problems I was good at solving and forget about the ones over which I had no control. Those problems were practical ones and they were the key to my survival. From an early age, I loved making things, finding out how things worked, moulding fragments of the world to my will. I had a prodigious imagination and imagined making extraordinary things. I also had the self-discipline to make it real. I couldn't solve the problem of senseless suffering. To this day, I can't watch a hospital scene on television where a life support machine is being turned off, without crying. I also can't listen to my partner telling me her problems without wanting to find a practical solution. While that may be irritating for her at times, for me it's the cornerstone of my survival and my success.

The biggest lesson my early life taught me was to know what you're good at and get better at it. This takes focus and self-discipline. It also takes humility and that's the most important lesson I've learned. When people look at leaders of any sort, they're quick to identify their extraordinary drive or sense of purpose. What is often overlooked or misunderstood is the humility it takes to be successful. Anyone who thinks they have nothing left to learn or even those who become leaders in their field and fall into complacency will always be overtaken by others. Humility means knowing there is always more to learn, that you can always be better at what you do, that there will be others who are better at doing what you do and from whom you can learn. It's a lesson that applies to anyone who wants to lead.

Practical problem- solving and design is a humbling process. I have come up with a hundred ideas that have failed for every one that works. I accept that ratio and so must anyone who wants to succeed. The secret is to see failures as problems that can be overcome and not as terminal blocks to progress. An example of this was when I went into the Dragon's Den and Theo Paphitis broke a strap hook on the Trunki. For me, there was an easy solution. For him, it was an insurmountable problem. That doesn't mean he isn't a good problem- solver. If he wasn't he wouldn't be one of the country's most successful entrepreneurs. It just means he missed a business opportunity. He will have missed others for the same reason. So have I. And so has every successful entrepreneur. As we move through life, we are taught, again and again, the same lesson: *be humble*.

Bad things, as Rabbi Harold Kushner pointed out in his famous book *When Bad Things Happen to Good People*, will happen to all of us. We have no control over that. We do, however, control how we play the cards we're dealt. In Kushner's case it was finding meaning in his son's illness. Kushner's son suffered from progeria, a rare genetic disorder which meant he aged much faster than normal children and died in his teens. For Kushner, the challenge was a spiritual one of how to sustain his faith in the face of such random injustice. For me, the challenge was a practical one: how could I use my fascination with product design to live the best life I am able to live. To people with a stronger emotional focus, this may seem like evasion. It's not. It's just another way of getting through the night – sometimes quite literally: my physiotherapy was done on a 'tipping bed', a medical looking frame and thin mattress that positioned me at a 20 degree incline while I 'percussed' my chest by tapping it to create vibrations to dislodge mucus off my lungs. So when I went to university I designed and built my own bed with hidden legs that swung out at the back to create the necessary incline. I also designed it to look like a normal bed, rather than a piece of medical equipment. A normal bed for a normal student leading a normal life.

From the outside, the story of my life can be defined as a story of survival against the odds or a story of how persistence and creativity can drive success. The story from the inside is very different. Survival and success are simply the by-product of my single-minded determination to focus on what I love doing and build my life around it. I do this by choosing which battles to fight and which to ignore, always doing my best (and often not succeeding) in keeping focused on what I can control and ignoring the rest. That, I believe, is the story of how lives can be well-lived and businesses built on firm foundations. It's a story and a struggle we all share. It's also the story of *why*, of finding meaning and purpose to keep us going when we risk being overwhelmed by circumstances beyond our control. For me, the story involved building a wall between me and the illness I was born with. It also involved a promise to live. It felt like the only path I could take but I'm sure there were others. There are no right answers, just an endless process of trial and error and an endless lesson in humility.

Astronauts and Spaceships

What do you do when you face an obstacle? Do you accept the limit or defy it?

Genetics and neuroscience have proved that we are not born as 'blank slates'. We bring into the world a greater or lesser tendency to be open, conscientious, agreeable, extroverted or emotionally stable. We are born healthy or with a genetic mutation that makes us sick. Our families will be rich or poor, living in peaceful or warring countries. We will have parental love to ourselves or have to share it with siblings and, as the psychologist John Bowlby claimed, every child has to answer the most fundamental question of all: is the world a safe place?

Random mutations and accidents of circumstance will, of course, create a world in which some things are easier to achieve than others. If your parents are doctors or lawyers, you are likely to have greater educational opportunity than if your parents are unemployed or in low-skilled jobs. If three nucleotides spanning positions 507 and 508 of the cystic fibrosis transmembrane conductance regulator on chromosome 7 are missing, then you will, like me and Kate, lack a single codon for the amino acid phenylalanine and your prognosis will be early death.

Clogged-up lungs, breathing difficulties and weakened immunity place limitations on my life. My attitude is to persist beyond anything reasonable in defying those limitations. As a child, I dreamed of being an astronaut until I found out that astronauts need strong, healthy lungs and good respiratory function. I wanted to be a soldier but soldiers also need strong lungs. Even as a child I had scant respect for limits and my response to these discoveries was to compound my ambition: if life said 'no', then I'd just have to prove life wrong. Of course, at some point, someone said, 'There's things you won't be able to do because you have cystic fibrosis, like being an astronaut and a soldier'.

Do you accept limits or defy them?

I refused to let the seeming impossibility of going into orbit or the prospect of an early death stop me dreaming. Instead of letting CF put a wall of limits around my life, I worried less about what I couldn't do and focused instead on what I could.

Of course, it's important to have dreams and to set yourself goals. Without them we have no direction and our world becomes smaller than it might otherwise be. However, dreams and goals must be specific. Much of our misery comes from thinking we can be anything, do anything or achieve anything without working out how we're going to do it. Unlimited power is a message the ego loves to hear but, unless the message is anchored in reality, it becomes corrosive and breaks our resilience. Having a dream of being rich without knowing what you have to do to achieve it is a sure guarantee of poverty.

It's also important to be passionate about what you do. The educationalist Sir Ken Robinson calls it finding your 'element' and, when you've found it, he advises you to work as hard as you can to build your life around it. That requires saying no to everything else, which means sacrificing other dreams you might have. Setting limits and boundaries, whether they are chosen freely or forced on us by circumstances beyond our control, are key components of success. This usually means outhitting your limitations like water outwits a barrier by going under or around it, cheating the barrier into a sense of victory, ignorant of the fact it's been breached.

Mostly, however, limitations are ugly.

My first experience of that ugliness was at infant school.

– Can you stay behind a moment please, Robert?

I looked at the teacher. I wanted to go out with the other children and play. She gestured for me to sit down at a table beside her desk.

– We think you need some extra help with reading and writing.

She was right. I struggled to read and my spelling ranged from pore to teribal.

– We have something that can help you, she said.

That 'Thing' turned out to be a tobacco tin full of cards I swiped through a terminal linked to a computer. Every card had words written on it and, when I swiped them, it spoke in a voice that made Stephen Hawking sound like he was speaking in received pronunciation:

- – A-P-P-L-E
- – C-A-R-A-V-A-N
- – T-O-R-T-O-I-S-E
- – I-D-I-O-T

I hated that voice. Having to practise my English kept me away from my friends and the whole exercise felt pointless because I knew why I was bad at English. I was dyslexic. I learned this years later, by accident, and I'm still not sure whether being undiagnosed is better than facing the humiliation of a label. In any event, labels are just another limit to be overcome, like the severely dyslexic writer A.A. Gill, who dictated his award-winning journalism. I don't have many regrets but one of them is I wish I could have read Gill's views on school failures when I was pigeon-holed as one of them: 'The interesting adults are always the school failures, the weird ones, the losers, the malcontents, this isn't wishful thinking. It's the rule.'

With or without a diagnosis or a pigeonhole, words didn't behave for me the way they did for other children. I was still reading Fuzzbuzz books when my friends were onto Roald Dahl and *The Secret Seven*. The 'thing' didn't make matters any better. It simply confirmed what I already knew and I just wanted it to shut up.

When I went to secondary school, the indignity continued and I was put in the special needs class twice a week to 'help you with your reading and writing, Robert'.

I hated that class more than I hated the voice from the tobacco tin. It was run by a teacher called Mrs Burden and her pupils were known as 'Burden's Babies'. These babies weren't like the famous Busby Babes, a team of talented world-beaters. We were babies because we were considered thick, beyond hope, a menagerie for other kids to stare at and be grateful they were on the right side of the line that divided us. We were also fodder for verbal bullying. If you've ever been bullied, you'll know that, beneath the bravado, the bully is weaker than you; otherwise, he wouldn't have to exploit your vulnerability to make himself feel strong. When you're facing the bully, however, that knowledge isn't at the front of your mind and, even if it is, it doesn't help. You just want the bullying to stop. It didn't help that I was also a poor communicator. People were problems I found much more difficult to solve than problems posed by materials like metal or plastic or wood. I also had a habit of interrupting people and saying exactly what I thought at inappropriate times.

I was, however, a Burden Baby and there was nothing I could do about it.

– You're one of the babies, Rob.

– If you weren't an idiot you wouldn't be in there, would you?

– Do you know how to spell 'cat'?

I was being punished for not being good at something over which I had little control. It was unfair, of course, but I never let myself become too preoccupied with fairness. The defect on chromosome 7 saw to that. I knew that, however much I improved my reading and writing, I'd still be a Burden Baby. Matters deteriorated further when they put me in a French class and started teaching me about adjectives and, my English never having progressed to any explanation of grammar, all I could think was 'What the hell is one of those?' I felt the same about adverbs and nouns. Quite how anyone expected me to learn a foreign language when I could barely read or write in English is beyond me.

There were other challenges too.

CF stunted my physical development and I was short for my age, which meant that 'basketball player' was another career choice that was not possible for me. As an act of defiance, I played the game a lot and Dad installed a hoop at home. I often invited my friend Gareth, who also suffered from CF, to come over and play basketball. We played and laughed like normal boys but we shared a 'label' and found refuge in each other's company. At the time, it was not known that CF sufferers should not mix because of the risk of cross-infection, so while we were shooting hoops we were also playing Russian Roulette with our lives. CF had taken a firmer hold of Gareth than me and I watched him waste away. Thin and pale, he died shortly after his 12th birthday.

So I grew up torn between wanting to belong and knowing I was different. That difference was about more than carrying an illness defined as terminal. My mind didn't work in the same way as everybody else's. I didn't deny that difference. I accepted it in the same way as, years later, I accepted Kate's death. This wasn't an act of heroism or calculated defiance. It was simply a realisation that, if my choices were more limited and my life likely to be shorter, then I had to drown in self-pity or, as my mother said, 'just get on with it'. I chose the latter.

Getting on with it meant finding ways to work around the limitations circumstances had imposed on me. I did that by seeing my life as a series of problems that had to be solved. I was good at solving them because I was good at identifying them. You can't solve a problem you don't know about. This, as Sir Ken Robinson would say, was my 'element'.

When I was a small child, perhaps three or four years old, I helped my Dad work on a derelict chapel he'd bought in Wales. During the holidays, he'd go there and restore it. Ivy wormed its way up the walls, partially covering the arched windows on the side of the chapel. Some people see prayers sunk in the walls of old chapels, especially Welsh ones. To me, the walls just needed repairing. That was a problem I could solve, more tangible than dead prayers. As I watched my father mix cement, I took a small shovel he'd given me and did my best to do the same. I just wanted to know how things worked, why they broke and how they could be fixed and made better than they were before. I watched my father work with hammers, chisels, all manner of tools including basic computer plotters. A highly skilled man, he'd built a business as a retail interior designer. One of his clients was Laura Ashley and he'd ask Kate and I to fold up store plans. He told us he needed the help. In truth, Mum just needed a break. Fascinated by exotic wallpaper and upholstery samples, I lost myself in a world of endless beauty and creativity. I loved the texture of the materials he worked with. By the time I was seven, I'd sculpted a face out of a block of wood and the pattern of my life was set.

Thanks to Lego, I'd also become a well-travelled astronaut. My journeys to distant galaxies began with earthbound experiments with Duplo bricks. From there I progressed quickly and soon I built spaceships and capsules to explore brave new worlds. There was no limit to what I could create. Whatever it was I was building, I'd read the instructions and follow them closely. Once the spaceship or machine or tower was complete, I dismantled it. When a mass of bricks and bits and pieces lay on the floor in front of me, I assembled and reassembled them in as many forms as I could. In this world, everything seemed possible. The limitations of CF or being short or struggling to read and spell dissolved into nothing as I moved the magical pieces into one shape then another, making and unmaking the world at will.

Before I went to secondary school, I used Lego to build cars with electric engines and gears. While instructions became more complex and the finished object more spectacular, that wasn't what kept me engaged. It was the *process* of creating, the feeling of total immersion that captivated me, a process and a feeling, a way of being, that was to govern my development as a child and my professional life as an adult. Creativity is about solving problems and the joy of doing that is in the process itself more than in the outcome. It allows me to shut the world out, to lose myself in the mechanics of my imagination and let the pain disappear. I work without a plan, just endless curiosity about where the process takes me. Where fear stifles and keeps us locked in prisons of our own making, curiosity breaks locks; it asks, 'What might happen?' without a wobble in our voice. It opens the vault of our creativity, where, if we look hard enough, we'll find things that other people can't see, like a Trunki.

As I grew older my fascination with the creative process deepened. I remember watching a documentary about the tightrope walker Philippe Petit. In 1974, just after the completion of the Twin Towers in New York, Petit, along with his friends, hatched an extraordinary plot to break into the North Tower, climb to the roof in the middle of the night and throw a tightrope between the two towers. The plan was for Philippe to walk between the towers, almost 1,500 feet above ground with no safety net, on the morning 7 August 1974. The result was a feat that amazed New Yorkers and stands as one of the greatest artistic achievements of the twentieth century. A police officer who arrived at the scene to arrest Petit watched him moving backwards and forwards between the towers, described him as a 'dancer'. Beyond the courage and determination it took to do this, what impressed me most was Petit's attitude to the challenge: 'It's impossible, that's for sure, so let's start working.'

If you are to create anything, first you dream, then you plan and, finally, you act, knowing that, as the Prussian Field Marshall Helmuth von Moltke the Elder said: Plans never survive contact with the enemy.' I identified with Petit's motivation. Both of us, facing death in our own way, turn away from our demons by absorbing ourselves in the creative process.

The end-point of that process is often ill-defined. On a cold December morning, shortly after Kate died, when snow lay thick on the ground, I decided to build something from snow and ice. I had no idea what I was going to create as I felt ice falling through my fingers, freezing my hands, the crunch of my boots in the snow and the wisps of my breath rising into the air, as I gathered and moulded the snow into what turned out to be an enormous Sphinx-like creature.

– That's extraordinary, Mum said when she saw it.

I laughed. It was just something I made. What, to me, was extraordinary was the process of making things like the battery-powered racing car I designed as an 11-year-old. The teacher asked us to design a child's toy with a motor. I got the idea from a friend who had a radio-controlled car. The result was a battery-powered racing car with a wooden structure and a vacuum-formed plastic shell. It took two weeks to complete. What struck me about this project wasn't the finished product, which I felt needed improving, but the fact that no-one in the class had thought of doing anything like this. They hadn't deviated from using wood and there was no indication of any problem-solving in the design and build process that involved stretching the limits of the brief. Every detail of the project was an opportunity to solve problems I didn't know I had when I began. Grand visions may be needed for inspiration but it's in the detail that creativity *works*. Solutions breed new problems and these animate the endless pro-cess of designing, building and refining. One of the many problems I failed to foresee was that the wooden wheels kept spinning as they turned instead of sticking firmly on the ground. At first, I couldn't think how to solve the problem until I stumbled on the idea of cutting up the inner tube of a bike and sticking the rubber pieces onto the wooden wheels. It solved the problem instantly.

At some point – I must have been about 13 – I came across a book by award-winning product designers Richard Seymour and Dick Pow-ell. Their photo-realistic visualisations, made with marker pens, of common products like kettles, irons and cars, flicked before me like a hypnotist's watch. Mesmerised, I borrowed my brother's Sony cas-sette player complete with microphone and used the techniques I'd learned in the book to bring it to life.

At 14, I designed a series of ride-on toys, which included a plane complete with propeller. I described it as

> a sit on plane for a young child, it is steerable and the propel-ler (sic) turns round with the back wheels. It would be about 600mm long and 200mm high. It would be painted like a spit fire (sic) and have the same camaflarged (sic) colours.

I also designed a train and created a working model for a ride-on dig-ger, which is still on display at my school.

The link between these early products and the global success of the Trunki ride-on suitcase is obvious and, having discovered something I loved, my passion for product design grew. At school I chose to focus on CDT (craft, design and technology) and turned being a Burden Baby to my advantage. Even the discarded and the written-off can find redemption on their own terms if we live, fluidly, like water. I didn't care that CDT was for the backward and academically deficient. Although I didn't know it at the time, I had Sir Ken on my side and I was in my 'element'. To date, Sir Ken's talk, *Do Schools Kill Creativity?* has over 60 million views and is the most watched TED Talk ever. Millions of people, who've seen their creativity killed by a kaleidoscope of assassins, from zealous administrators to the industrial machinery of sets and grades, have listened to Sir Ken and found a way to express themselves.

I was the only pupil in the entire school who chose CDT for A level. Destined to be top and bottom, best and worst, in a class of one, I indulged my passion for cycling and designed a recumbent bike called Prodigy, and a bike stand, which could be used to secure a bike on the ground for performing maintenance or on the roof of a car. Driven to make something that could be cast from my imagination into the real world and still work, I made the stand from metal and welded the parts together. The recumbent bike came from a desire to find new ways to express my passion for cycling. I loved the aerodynamic Lotus track bike, designed by Mike Burros, that Chris Boardman rode to Olympic gold in Barcelona in 1992. I was drawn to recumbents because they're the outsiders of the cycling world, despite being faster and more aerodynamic than road bikes. I also used fibreglass to sculpt a seat not a saddle, which nestled comfortably against the rider's back. I went straight to the top of the class.

In addition to CDT, I studied maths and physics at A level. Physics, like CDT, provided me with an endless supply of fascinating problems I solved by calculating and measuring, such as finding out the gravitational force between the earth and the moon, the relative velocities of objects escaping from Earth's atmosphere or the time it took for the mucus on my lungs to move from body to bowel.

No man is an island and neither is a boy who taps his chest like a demented drummer before he goes to school. I'm as grateful now for the company of friends and strangers as I was then to see other pupils in my maths and physics A level classes. Company creates the illusion of normality, yet I still had this determination, bordering on the obsessive, to follow my own path. That gave me a freedom my peers didn't have. There's nothing that puts more shackles on your life than needing to be liked to the point where you organise your life around who other people think you should be rather than who you are. Honesty, for me, was more of a practical virtue than a moral one: the price of lying to myself about who I was seemed like a ridiculous and costly thing to do.

The ghosts were still with me.

During my A levels I thought of Kate alive and banished thoughts of her lying, motionless, on a hospital bed. When your twin sibling dies of an illness that's supposed to kill you and you look in the mirror, you need to see life not death. It's a practical approach to grief, decluttered of stages you're meant to pass through and I remember, not long after Kate died, overhearing my mother talking on the telephone. I only heard one side of the conversation but it wasn't difficult to make out what was going on:

> I feel I spent so much time with Kate because she was much sicker than Rob . . . Yes, I do . . . He puts on a good show, but I'm sure he feels it deeply . . . I hate thinking of him struggling underneath it all . . .

She was right. I put on a good show. I buried my emotions so deep, they became strangers, wild things that snapped and bit inside me, so I kept them at a distance. One of the ways I did that was to process my emotions through other people. Especially Mum. I loved drawing and, shortly after Kate's death, when Mum's distress was overwhelming for both of us, I drew her a picture of Kate. I loved the play of light and dark I got when I drew with pencils and I wanted the picture of Kate to be as close to photo-realism as I could get. Even in my attempts to ease Mum's pain, I was refining my skills, finding life in a portrait of death.

It was hard, too, during my A Levels, to see Mum unable to change a single detail in Kate's room. When I was at school I blotted everything out, kept the wall between me and my illness intact, but when I got home Kate's room chipped away at the mortar, always threatening to let something ugly through. That room remained unchanged for a decade after she died. It was Mum's way of managing her grief. Even Kate's Forever Friends lay lifeless on the bed. Mum did her best to protect me from her grief but how could she when *her* feelings felt more real to me than my own? When the emotional substance of your life belongs to someone else, watching them suffer is torture.

I craved normality.

Throughout my childhood, the idea of normality was like a panacea, a bulwark against CF. I had three ways of creating and sustaining normality:

> Focusing on what I could do and not worrying about what I couldn't.
> Doing what I could do with focus and incredible self-discipline.
> Keeping my feelings about problems I couldn't solve to myself.

Those three behaviours have followed me throughout my life. They are the cornerstone of my success and the bricks in the wall that keep my illness under control. Like all behaviours, they have a dark side, especially the one about keeping feelings to myself. The next funeral I went to after Kate's was my grandfather's. I was at university and his death was sad without being tragic, a 'good death' that lets you celebrate the life that came before it. I expected a restful solemnity but, when I saw my mother crying, the wall collapsed, not a few chunks of mortar or the odd brick falling away, the whole thing shattered in an instant and I wailed uncontrollably. I was at two funerals at once, my grandfather's where the young live and the old pass away, and a nastier funeral, my sister's, the one I'd buried, where the conveyor belt that takes us all to the cemetery gets broken into bits, where young and old forget their place in the order of things. I remember people staring at me, relatives who knew, strangers who didn't. I willed myself to stop but the tears kept coming, a problem without a solution and all I wanted to do was run. But where to?

Overcoming obstacles takes, at the very least, some basic navigation tools. In the Cubs I loved the challenge of being out with a group of friends, having to make my way using a compass and a map, often having to sleep outdoors and deal with inclement weather, taking my medication, doing my physiotherapy, spitting mucus onto roads and roses. What I loved most was working with a plan and testing it against the variables of nature. I might not have been swimming with crocodiles or climbing the north face of the Eiger, but I had a task which involved solving problems and that was enough.

Perhaps inspired by experience with the Scouts and driven by the need people defined as *abnormal* have to prove their hyper-normality (or normal life with a rocket up its arse), I resolved, aged 10, to sleep in a tent in the garden for a month. My parents expected me to give up after a night or two. I didn't. I kept going and would have made it were it not for a nightmare I had two days before the end of the month. Terrified, I leapt up in my sleeping bag and shone my torch through a gap in the tent. The light reflected off the eyes of the cows in the next field and their luminous strength mingled with the memory of my nightmare led to a sudden panic and I escaped into the house. I gave up, two days short of my target.

Hyper-normality is another world for denial. *I am not sick. I do not have CF. I am not spilling my lungs. I will live a normal life.* To prove the point, I took up mountain biking. Immersion in the adrenaline release of biking down steep hills and across rugged terrain fulfilled my hunger for life. I took up athletics and became one of the fastest middle distance runners at my school and, although I fared less well at county level, I knew if I trained hard enough I'd get better and if I got better I'd get good and, if I got good, I could do something remarkable, which I did. Later in life, I ran marathons and became an accomplished middle distance runner and a triathlete, pushing my lungs to the limit, the same lungs made to kill me in my teenage years. Even now, when I cross a finishing line, clogged up and struggling to breathe, having pushed my body beyond all reasonable limits, I'm screaming, 'Fuck you, CF!' I'm knocking on a door with a plaque on the outside, Denial or Survival, I'm never sure which – but when it opens it takes me past the limits of the mutation on chromosome 7.

Would I have chosen this path if I'd been given a choice? Probably not. I've got the life I've got and if I hadn't been born with CF, stuck in special needs classes, watched my twin sister die, hated my mum's pain, then I might never have known the difference between problems that can be solved and those that can't. That wisdom, which I did nothing to acquire other than to be born with the injustice of a pre-natal death sentence, was the making of me. It gave me focus and a determination to defy the odds in everything I did.

Learning to focus on what you can control is an essential skill in life and business. Take a moment to think of all the time you've wasted trying to control other people or moaning about how difficult your life is because you haven't got enough money or because people have let you down. When that happens, the best thing you can do is to separate those elements of the problem that you can change from those that you can't. If you get that judgement wrong, your chances of success and serenity are severely limited.

Our focus is also weakened by the insistence of our ego that it knows best. It doesn't, and the longer it takes us to learn that lesson, the more entrenched and inflexible our behaviour becomes. By a stroke of luck, genetic and circumstantial, I've never been afraid to see my own flaws. If life is a problem to be solved and I am a part of life, then I, too, am a problem to be solved. Or, more accurately, I'm an endless series of problems to be solved, where every solution is obsolete at the moment I figure it out. The wire-walker Philippe Petit saw this fluidity as the essence of creativity. He said:

> Life should be lived on the edge of life. You have to exercise rebellion: to refuse to tape yourself to rules, to refuse your own success, to refuse to repeat yourself, to see every day, every year, every idea as a true challenge – and then you are going to live your life on a tightrope.

I've had the privilege of meeting many successful people and the one quality they share is a relentless determination to make the best of their talents. Determination, however, without focus is blind. There is no doubt that a man like Philippe Petit could have succeeded at many things. His drive and intelligence are formidable. Yet, it was the first time he stepped on a tightrope that he knew he was in his 'element'. That's the way I feel when I explore how products can be improved or problems solved through what feels like a process of almost perpetual failure until you arrive at a solution that works.

Focus, then, means learning a key skill, which is to know what you don't want to know or do. Imagine you're standing in a vast library.

There are millions of books on more floors than you can count. In a single lifetime, the maximum number of books an adult can read is in the low thousands, unless they're a Burden Baby when the number decreases to the low teens. The key to knowledge, then, is knowing which books to pick up and which to discard. This is, of course, a risky business. The advent of the internet has seen people narrow their interests and points of reference, so they'll only accept ideas from people that think like they do and believe in the same things. It's vital to be open to learning from as many people as you can, especially if their ideas are different from yours. We stop ourselves becoming victims of our own inflexibility by being open to new ideas and being able to narrow that focus down so we can fuel our creativity.

If understanding the power of focus and finding your 'element' are essential to personal and professional development, then self-discipline is the means to make them real. Most businesses fail not through a lack of talent or focus but from the absence of the relentless work ethic and self-discipline needed to keep evolving. Darwin defined the fittest members of any species as the most flexible because flexibility means more behavioural choices. If you don't get the balance right between focusing on what you do and evolving your skills and the products and services your business sells, then you'll fail.

To me, talent means the skills you develop when you work hard at something. Your genes and your environment can work for or against you in many ways, but if you keep working at something, whatever that thing is, then you'll get better at it.

The final part of the self-development puzzle is managing your emotions. For me that's easier than most, because I find it easy to block things out and keep focused on problems I can solve. When I tell people that I went to the pub when I got back to Loughborough University the night after my sister died, they look at me as if trying to work out how I could block that much pain out. They don't ask me anything about it but, if they did, my answer would be the same every time: I went out not because Kate dying didn't matter or because I didn't love her but *because she mattered too much*.

Despite what so much popular personal and business psychology tells us, there's no right or wrong way of doing things. There are simply ways that work and ways that don't. Knowing the difference between the two in my life has helped me overcome many challenges. My parents taught me if I wanted more money, then I had to work. I did my first paper round as a 12-year-old. I then worked at weekends cleaning and stacking reclaimed bricks and driving a forklift truck at a brick and slate company. I also worked at the Tesco cigarette counter, which was ironic because CF meant I couldn't smoke and the only way I identified the different brands was by the colour of the packets. However, the best job I ever got was when my father commissioned me to design and build an office desk. The finished product was inspired by a coffee table I created called Bug. For the desk, I scaled up the insect legs and finished it with a glass top. I also made chairs and a meeting table to match. As with everything I create, all I could see were ways of making it better but, more than 25 years later, that table is still the one my Dad uses in his study and I still want to improve it.

A final thought on work: there's an ever-expanding book called *Diagnostic and Statistical Manual of Mental Disorders* (now in its fifth edition). It grows year-on-year as psychiatrists seek the honour of an emotional dysfunction named after them. In the book, workaholism is defined as 'being overly concerned about work, driven by an uncontrollable work motivation, and to investing so much time and effort to work that it impairs other important life areas'. What this misses is that intense focus, by definition, enhances some things and depletes others but that doesn't mean the great Victorian asylums should be rebuilt to cater for people who, at various times in their lives, work excessively. Dad taught me to work hard. Sir Ken taught me the importance of finding my 'element'. My life is a blend of those two influences. I may never be an astronaut or a soldier, but I know what it is to be immersed in what I do and to keep going where others falter. It's the key to my success and my survival.

Horizons
and Habits

I n the shape-shifting world of our imagination, the symbolism of the horizon is anchored, as Roosevelt said, in 'the hope, the belief, the conviction that there is a better life, a better world, beyond the horizon'. Yet hopes are uncertain, beliefs malformed and convictions swayed by sharp wounds and inclement weather. Faced with these tricks of our imagination, horizons expand and contract our lives, serving both as limits and the absence of all limits, as symbols of pure possibility and the confinement of that possibility within the walls of a prison cell. So, I watched from the beach as my father and Kate disappeared behind a large rock, the sound of their oars cutting through the water, fading into nothing. A little under five years before Kate died, it was a family holiday full of simple pleasures, untroubled by fear. The line that cut sea from sky was barely visible and everything was open, pregnant with the future. Yet, when that tiny rowing boat vanished out of sight and the gentle rolling of the sea swallowed their laughter, I looked into the distance and felt the horizon pressing on me like a limit, a laugh become a cough, living breath become a dead lung.

Another horizon. Ibiza. Eighteen months after Kate died. I finished my A levels and travelled with friends for a week-long celebration. We danced on the beach, drinking, laughing. I turned to raise a glass to the sun when the blue expanse closed like a clam, snapping at my youth, yelling that I'm far from home, without my support network or a familiar hospital. When I felt myself struggle for breath I heard the splash of old oars cutting through the water and Kate's laughter bursting the self-important bubble of my fear.

Horizons may set a limit to what our eyes can see, while opening the limitless reservoir of our imagination. I can't be an astronaut, live a life free from cystic fibrosis or laugh with my sister again but, in a single moment, I can imagine extraordinary products and push towards a kaleidoscope of possible futures. In that moment I can do anything and the tension between doing and seeing frames our lives and our businesses: if we have the courage to break the habits that bind us and see beyond the present horizon of our lives, almost anything is possible.

My approach to product design and running a business is driven by a defiant determination to refuse any limits to my creativity. I may not be able to make every product I conceive or succeed at everything I do, but no-one can take away from me the freedom of my imagination. Like the Queen in *Alice Through the Looking Glass*, I've believed as many as six impossible things before breakfast and I'll keep doing that until I die of old age or failed lungs, whichever comes first.

My first commercial experience of the power of habits to block our vision came when I designed the first Trunki in 1997, in my second year at university. The path to that design began during the first year of my A levels when I visited Newcastle to decide whether I was going to study civil engineering or product design. Cities entice and often disappoint. Newcastle didn't. It may be, as Alan Rickman claimed, that 'every English actor is nervous of a Newcastle accent' but I was drawn to the industrial history of the city with its seven bridges, bellowing chimneys, polished locomotives, steam turbines, hydraulic cranes and orphaned ships fashioned by lost generations of shipbuilders. What did it matter if I couldn't understand a word they said, when I loved the breadth of their ingenuity?

The poet Philip Larkin once said he moved to Hull, which he described as a 'fish smelling dump', because its proximity to nowhere meant he was left largely undisturbed to write. Newcastle appealed to me because its distance from home gave me freedom to build a life for myself. It was far enough away from the parents I loved to take my damaged lungs, wash them in the smoke-stacked waters of the River Tyne and learn to breathe on my own terms. Without giving this gift of my own life to myself, how could I possibly give anything of value to anyone else? So, moving to the city was one of the keys to my survival. Solving intractable design problems requires immersion in my own imagination and the translation of that imagination into functional products. While that process is collaborative, it begins with an obsessive solitariness that's best lived in busy cities. Fields and sheep may be fuel for poets. Product designers need human company.

My first appointment was at Newcastle University. I didn't have any expectations about what might happen. Even then, as a 17-year-old boy, I knew there was a gulf that divided real from imagined experiences, so expecting anything was a guarantee of disappointment. On the way into Newcastle, I passed the Angel of the North, a work of art I adore, which serves as a homage to the city's past and a sleepless witness to its future. The energy of the city was palpable and vibrant, yet as soon as I saw the traditional, imposing university building, it didn't feel like a place I could belong. I needed an institution facing forwards, not skulking behind a grand facade.

– It's in there and down the stairs, the porter said, pointing.

I found the staircase and wound my way down to the basement. The first thing that struck me was the pungent smell. Formaldehyde perhaps. The room I entered was windowless, the atmosphere stagnant. A smattering of students stood behind workstations, dressed in white coats. A man approached me. Mid-40s. A kind face. He extended his hand without smiling. Conversation was difficult. I remember two lines:

– What will I be doing for most of the course? I asked.
– Testing concrete, he replied.

I'm sure I asked more and he said more. Civil engineering is about more than testing concrete and I have no doubt that the standards at the department were high, as was the calibre of the students. But that's not how experience works. We base most of our decisions on extraneous factors. Whether or not the room had windows and whether the professor who guided me was an introvert or extrovert was of no significance to the academic credentials of the department. It was, however, decisive in my decision not to take that course.

I took a 20-minute walk from Newcastle University to Northumbria University. Towers of metal and glass took the place of Gothic facades. I walked along paths, past trees and came to a red-brick building. I climbed to the second floor and inside the walls were covered, floor to ceiling, in consumer products designed by students. A video phone caught my eye as did a name on the wall: Jonathan Ive. The university's most famous alumnus began his journey to Apple from this university. Other fascinating products flashed before me. It felt like walking onto the set of a science-fiction movie. There was no longer any doubt that here, among the speculative creativity of product designers, was where I belonged. This was my 'element'.

– You must be Rob.

– Yes.

– I'm Mr Waters, your course director and I'm pleased to meet you.

He shook my hand and took me into a bright room, purpose- built for product design. It smelled airy, not a trace of formaldehyde. The students smiled at me. I smiled back.

– This is where we design the future, he said.

I spoke to some of the students, fully equipped with tools and machines to turn imaginary designs into working models. They designed an array of consumer products from computers to hand-held devices. Above all, I remember their passion. Newcastle University was spread throughout the city. Northumbria University, in contrast, felt like a self-contained hub of activity.

– We also send our students on work placements abroad, the man said.

– Where to?

– New York, San Francisco, Hong Kong, pretty much anywhere.

I was hooked.

The interview went well. I presented my designs for the bike stand and the recumbent bike.

– You've clearly got talent, one of the interviewees said, but it's more technical than creative. If you want to get accepted we recommend you do an art foundation course first.

I didn't want to live at home for another year but I had a simple choice: either I wanted to be on this course or I didn't. It was an easy decision to make. I went back home and a year later I returned to Northumbria University to begin a degree course in product design.

I had two rules:

1. Learn
2. Have fun

At school I was Robert, a Burden Baby with a chronic illness. At university I was Rob, a product designer with a passion for all-night parties. The first thing I learned was that creativity and pleasure serve the same master. Long nights spent in pubs, wine bars or techno-clubs are the mirrored twin of nights spent hunched over a workstation, a single-minded hunger to *live*, to prove to myself that I had a future.

Years of weightlifting, running and cycling meant I was fitter than most of my peers. In bars, on the track, in a design studio, I matched them all. Some of my friends called me Duracell. The real demon, of course, was CF. I was alive or not dead yet, depending on whether my mood was optimistic or hungover with pessimism. Either way, when you don't know how long you have to live, when my lungs might resign without notice, I chose to drain each day of its life, leave nothing on the field of play, as Alan Shearer might have said. There were many times when bad lungs and good times didn't mix. I didn't care. I'd rather die playing than live fearfully.

From the moment the course began, my passion for product design consumed me. Oscar Wilde wrote in the preface to *The Picture of Dorian Gray*, that 'all art is useless' because it serves no purpose other than its own invention. Product design, architecture or engineering, on the other hand, drive action. Unlike a painting, their meaning isn't stuck in a solipsistic box. They have purpose, they have to *work*.

I revelled in the collaborative aspect of my work, of being with like-minded students from product design or other creative disciplines like photography, graphics and fashion. Finding the right balance between following your own path and allowing input from others is the key to creative and commercial success: if you are too rigid and closed in on yourself then you'll miss opportunities to learn and develop; you'll also stunt your development if you're too open and let yourself be blown in any number of directions depending on who you speak to.

I've always felt the power of peer groups in my life and, in the same year I began my undergraduate degree, a psychologist called Judith Rich Harris made one of the discoveries that I've found easy to connect with. Like me, she was an outsider. Despite being a graduate of Harvard University, she was barred from doing a PhD in psychology by George A. Miller, the chair of the department. Justifying his decision, he simply told her that he did not consider her intelligent enough to proceed. In a wonderful irony, more than 35 years later she won the George A. Miller prize for her contribution to behavioural genetics. Her main discovery was to prove that peer groups play a more significant developmental role than parents. Whilst I've always been close to my parents and grateful for everything they gave me, the pivotal role of peer groups always made sense to me. If you don't feel nervous or exposed when you express your ideas to someone else, then you're talking to the wrong peer. If you have total confidence that your friend or colleague won't change your mind in any way, then you're not going to learn anything from them and you might as well talk to yourself. For me, the real tragedy of the way the internet has developed isn't that it connects people but that it feeds us more of the same type of content and drives us into ever-narrower interest groups that serve to reinforce what we already believe. True creativity and real personal growth demands that you expose yourself to people who know more than you do, whose opinion matters to you and who are able to *change what you think and what you do*.

In order to be open to criticism and new ideas, I've always tried (sometimes failing miserably) to be critical of my own work, to 'refuse my own success', as Philippe Petit put it. Again, when you get self-critical, like when you choose your peer groups, you have to be careful how you do it. For too many people, self-criticism means beating yourself up or getting overwhelmed by negative self-talk about how useless you are. That gets you nowhere. Effective self-criticism simply means you never reach a point where you are so sure of yourself that you close yourself up to being challenged.

My big life lesson in how peer groups, criticism and the intrusion of new ideas into a settled worldview can open or close the horizons of your life came during my second year at university. BASF, a global plastics manufacturer, ran a national competition to design an original piece of luggage. To many people, designing luggage may seem like a rather mundane task. To me, it was exciting and challenging. Creating consumer products involves technical, practical and psychological challenges. Above all, it presents you with problems that have multiple solutions and I was always determined to find the best one. In pursuit of this, I focused on what I could do, always mindful of getting feedback from people whose opinions I trusted, who shared the same 'element'. My strategy had three phases:

Research.
Planning.
Execution.

The research began in the luggage department at Fenwick in Newcastle city centre. The walls and floors were stuffed with the usual kaleidoscope of luggage brands. I picked up one suitcase after another. Large or small, from Carlton to Samsonite, they were all variations on the same theme: hard, moulded, plastic, functional, dull.

An assistant asked me if I wanted anything.

– Inspiration, I replied.

– Where do you want to travel?

– As far away from here as I can get.

The assistant opened a few suitcases. We talked about capacity and handles and durability. Never once did either of us mention aesthetics. Luggage was, after all, just luggage: purely functional.

Exhausted and devoid of ideas, I wandered into the toy department. I didn't have any children nor did I want to buy any toys. All I wanted was to be around kids with their chaotic, instinctive likes and dislikes. Above all, I needed to be around their fearlessness. Kids try something and if it doesn't get their attention, they move on. If they like a toy they'll play with it endlessly until something better comes along. That's why I love being around children. I share their spontaneity, their love of constant experimentation, their openness to new ideas. The colours and sounds of the toy department were a world away from the dense black and brown landscape of the luggage department. As a child, one of my brother's favourite toys was a green tractor. He drove it endlessly around the garden. It had a seat that lifted up to reveal a space big enough to store an apple. All ride-on toys shared this same problem: a lack of storage space. When children unleash their imagination, they need props. While make-believe props often do the job, how much better would it be if their ride-on toys stored real props? Then they'd be luggage and global transporters of a child's imagination. Out of nowhere, I had the idea of putting a ride-on toy and a suitcase together in a single product. It seemed a way to blend fun, functionality and aesthetics. It was also a cure for boredom at airports that didn't involve tears, tantrums or a sudden loss of the parental will to live. I felt that children would understand what I was doing and they'd drag their jaded parents, for whom the association of travel, time and children was irretrievably miserable, along with them.

In the days that followed, I planned out my route to the creation of the product. The moulding technology used on adult suitcases provided the necessary strength and lightness to be used on a ride-on dream carrier for kids. The main challenge I faced was how to ensure it was easy to manoeuvre and had sufficient storage space. I sketched a woolly mammoth design. It had long horns at the front for the child to hold onto and was covered in fur. I knew the fur would have to go eventually but I was getting lost in the fun of the product, just another child with a dream.

Long hours and late nights passed as I wrestled with the considerable design challenges the product posed. Eventually, I made a solid, scale model out of medium-density fibreboard, painted it and photoshopped kids on the back of it. I called it the Rodeo Ride-on Suitcase. Encouraged by feedback from my colleagues and tutors at the university, some of it raising design problems I hadn't thought of yet – let alone solved – I built a full-sized model to test on real children. The benchmark was for the child to have fun and be free from injury. In those days before computer-aided design, prototyping involved taking a big chunk of building insulation foam and sculpting it using hot wire cutters and sandpaper. This gave me the form of a product, without wheels and storage. It was good enough to test for ergonomics and a child's ability to propel itself forward without getting impaled on the horns of a woolly mammoth.

Mr Bailey, my course tutor, liked it. A few days later, Eden his daughter, a bright girl, four or five years old, came with him to the studio.

I didn't know what to expect but I was astonished at what she did.

She walked into the studio, looked bewildered for a few seconds, saw the prototype, ran over to it and sat on it. That moment, more than any other, was the most important on my journey from a basic prototype to a global brand. For the first time, I saw the ride-on suitcase through a child's eyes. Later on, I saw the same product through the weary, habit-formed eyes of product buyers, but now I saw how instinctive it was for a child.

– How did you know what to do? I asked.

– Do what? she replied distractedly.

– Just sit on it.

– What else am I supposed to do?

I laughed.

Designing products for kids is wonderful because their response is honest and immediate. Miriam just knew what the product was and how to use it, without anyone having to explain it to her. I kicked myself for not seeing how intuitive it was for kids. I now knew I'd conceived a product unlike anything in the luggage market, a product the target audience grasped easily. In some of my initial sketches I'd designed a semicircular indentation on the side of the product, like a flap on a horse's saddle, which became part of the visual DNA of Trunki.

On 5 May 1998 I got a letter from BASF telling me I'd got through to the final six in the national competition. They invited me to attend the final judging on 19 May. Four years after Kate died, at 20 years of age, I was on the cusp of winning my first design award.

The days between 5 and 19 May 1998 passed in a flurry of preparation. Whether through my genetics or personal experience of unexpected loss, I kept a cool head despite the anticipation. I had to deliver a 20-minute presentation to a panel of plastic industry experts. I worked on it meticulously, preparing for every eventuality.

One problem I had to solve was how the wheels were attached to the case. I solved it by taking apart a Dyson cylinder vacuum cleaner, finding out how the wheels were attached and using that as inspiration for attaching the wheels to my ride-on suitcase.

I ran through the presentation with Mr Bailey. He suggested a few amends. I made most of them and then I relaxed. All I could was my best and nothing more.

On the day of the judging, I focused on the product, the problems it was designed to solve and how it solved them.

– The problem children have when they're travelling, especially in airports, is they get bored. The problem their parents have is keeping them entertained. This ride-on suitcase solves both these problems.

I'd prepared well and I was sure of my ground. I spoke with confidence. My lungs were on their best behaviour and I didn't cough once. The judges seemed impressed.

After all six finalists gave our presentations, we had to wait until mid-afternoon for the result. I'd seen the other products and heard their presentations. Despite my desire to win, my main interest was simply in seeing what the other students had designed, thinking how I might solve a similar problem.

– You've all done extremely impressive presentations, the lead judge began. However, there is one design, which for its originality and commercial potential, stands apart from the rest. The winner is Rob Law for his ride-on suitcase.

After the presentation of the trophy and the photographs, one of the judges took me aside and said he thought this was a product that might be licensed by a manufacturer. That was all I needed to hear.

I had done more than win a competition. My horizons expanded from the university to the world of business and anything seemed possible.

A week after the final, I received a letter from the chairman of the Institute of Materials who chaired the plastics design committee. He wrote: 'I am passing your name on to two of my friends who may be interested in interviewing you with the possibility of offering you a position in their companies.'

One of the companies was Carlton International plc. Within weeks I was sitting before the technical director at Carlton pitching my ride-on suitcase as a piece of luggage. I brought a revised presentation board and prototype with me. They listened. I felt their enthusiasm. They clearly understood the viability of taking my idea to manufacture.

I was wrong.

With indecent haste, just a few minutes after I finished the presentation, I received my first rejection: 'We make luggage and I'm afraid your ride-on suitcase is a toy, so we won't be proceeding further.'

Of course, I was disappointed but, like with the rally car I made at school and the meeting with Dragons that was still a few years in the future, my main emotion was one of incomprehension: how can they not see what I can see?

I didn't dwell long on that rejection nor did I wallow in being the victim of a judgement that was outside my control. In rejecting me, they'd simply given me another opportunity: if I'd created a toy and not a piece of luggage then I'd sell the idea to a toy manufacturer.

I contacted several companies. In every case the meeting went well, they loved the product and then they rejected it. Some of the rejections were instant, others took weeks and one took 21 months, but the reason was always the same: 'We make toys and I'm afraid your ride-on suitcase is a piece of luggage, so we won't be proceeding further.'

I felt like Henry Ford and his 'faster horse'. It was clear I'd designed a product that solved a problem but didn't mirror any existing solution, which brings me back to horizons and habits. To push beyond the limits of any horizon, you have to take a risk with your imagination.

This is more difficult than it seems.

Most of the judgements and decisions we make in our lives are based on our habits, ways of seeing that have become so much a part of our behaviour, we assume they can't be changed. It's easy to recognise these fixed ways of seeing, since they tend to be accompanied by phrases like 'That's just the way I am' or 'I've always done things this way' or 'It's you that needs to change, not me'. Above all, habits are a way of justifying inaction. If we think our identity is fixed, then how can we change significantly, even if we wanted to? And why should we?

Yet these beliefs inhibit our personal and professional growth as we succumb to habits like these:

The Cannibal Habit develops when any new experience is absorbed into old ones, blinding us to the possibility of seeing anything new. It was, without doubt, the favourite habit of luggage and toy manufacturers. When they saw a ride-on suitcase, they chewed over the details, swallowed hard, choked on the horns and, when the grim digestion was over, saw either a toy or a piece of luggage, being incapable of seeing both.

The Love at Last Sight Habit isn't necessarily about love, although it can be, when, on the cusp of abandoning all hope, we settle on the most available possible partner. This happens because we're *lazy thinkers, usually preferring not to think at all, so we absorb a piece of information, such as an ill-informed opinion about the importance of strap hooks (see the chapter about Dragons) and, rather than wrestle with this information, we let it determine our subsequent behaviour. Put simply, the last thing we see or hear tends to have an irrational importance in our decision-making.*

The Damn Fool Habit *is a dogged way to waste to your money and your life. It comes from W.C. Fields, who said: 'If at first, you don't succeed, try, try again. Then quit. There's no use being a damn fool about it.' Except, of course, we're determined to be the damnest fools we can be, clutching to the prospect that our plans and projects will come good just because we've invested time, money, perhaps our entire life, in them. This is the biggest reason business investors lose their money: rather than pull a failing investment, they invest more because they're not prepared to admit the loss of what they've already sunk into their business.*

The Dig Your Heels In Habit *develops when we believe things that are clearly against our interests and, faced with the horror of being called stupid, we greet every attempt to get us to change our minds with a deepening attachment to our original belief and the behaviours that flow from it: think about Welsh sheep farmers who voted for Brexit or single-minded product designers suffering from CF who have a poor life expectancy, run marathons and party all night in the belief they're going to live long and prosper – that they might actually do so is merely the exception that proves the rule.*

These habitual ways of seeing the world limit our horizons trap us inside our own minds and usually lead to undesirable outcomes. How successful we are depends in large part on being able to recognise and overcome these ways of seeing. The consequences of not doing so make us intolerant and incapable of personal or professional growth.

They're also what stops us seeing new things and thinking in new ways, which is the essence of creativity: 'It's either a piece of luggage or it's a toy, it can't be both!'

They were wrong: it *was* both and I knew it. It was just a matter of biding my time and knocking on enough doors. While I pursued my dream of taking my ride-on suitcase into production, I continued with my degree, which ended with the creation of Flo, a reclining chair with movable platforms big enough for a laptop and Tact, a futuristic device that enabled lovers to communicate remotely through touch. Yet, it was the three work placements that gave me a sharp lesson on the importance of testing ideas in real-work environments.

At times, these experiences mirrored those with the luggage and toy manufacturers. I developed ideas that went nowhere because my boss didn't like it or didn't think it was commercially viable, without ever giving me a reason why. Undaunted, I used what spare time I had to knock on as many doors as I could to see how different design consultancies worked. I took a summer placement in New York just as the iMac was launched and the VW Beetle was relaunched. In product design, anything seemed possible. I set up meetings with leading product design companies and took every Friday afternoon off to attend them. I loved the open plan offices in old warehouses with their exposed brick and vaulted ceilings. Inspirational working environment, they freed people to be creative and express themselves. Years later, they also inspired the design of my own offices.

Living abroad was challenging for my CF but essential for my creative development. After graduation, I got a job at a Chinese productivity centre near Taipei in Taiwan where one of the first things I did was create a new product: *Sacrificial Underpants*. CF sufferers have a complex relationship with food. I was eight before I ate any fat. The overnight transition from 'no-fat' to 'full-fat' was thanks to a drug named Creon that replaces enzymes the pancreas doesn't produce because of CF. It gave me more strength to fight the illness because my body absorbed more nutrients. However, I wasn't the only benefi-ciary. It brought to an end one of the many logistical nightmares Mum had to deal with. Before Creon, if there was a children's birthday party, Mum phoned the organiser to make sure there was fat-free food myself and Kate could eat. Her aim wasn't just my physical health. She wanted me to go to a party with at least a semblance of normality. Often, this was difficult. The only cheese I could eat was Edam, which meant pineapple and cheddar cocktail sticks became pineapple and Edam cocktail sticks. The other kids didn't notice. I did. Then there were Weetabix cakes, which have entered CF mythol-ogy and the least said about them the better, except to say that they were as horrific as they sound.

However, oily food is still a problem for me and in Taiwan and many parts of China, toilets were a hole in the ground and toilet paper was not considered necessary as the oily food ensured a smooth evacu-ation. For me, it was rather more challenging and toilet paper turned out to be essential, which is why I invented *Sacrificial Underpants*. Once sacrificed, of course, underpants can't be reused, which meant I went 'commando' in many meetings, with all the grit but none of the glory of a soldier. As if to reward my secret courage, I was pre-sented during one meal with a local delicacy: a 1,000-year-old egg, matured for many months in horse urine. The result, predictably, was the sacrifice of another pair of underpants in a dimly lit room with battered metal walls and a hole in the ground into which I sunk my pants like a flag. Years later, when I manufactured Trunkis in China, there was a dramatic increase in *Sacrificial Underpants,* which served as a novel *memento mori*. During one visit to Dongguan in 2009 to launch Trunki Mk 3, the applause and celebrations were interspersed by flag-planting in a wide variety of holes-in-the-ground. In hindsight, I struggle to see what the greater success was: getting to a hole in time or launching a global product. Either way, *Sacrificial Underpants* are the perfect correction to rampant egotism: *Vanity of vanities*, says the Book of Ecclesiastes, *All is vanity*.

The pattern of unexplained rejections continued, only this time it was worse than ever. Continually pushed by my boss to come up with ideas, I designed what felt like an endless stream of consumer products, which included a telescope for bird watching, drinking water machines and hands-free kits for mobile phones. I didn't communicate much with the rest of the team because they didn't speak English very well and I can't speak Mandarin. Stuck in my role as what I jokingly called 'in-house design slave', I got inspiration from magazines scattered about the office. I couldn't stare out of the window for inspiration because our office was windowless, which added to my sense of physical and creative claustrophobia.

The ideas I created were presented at more than two dozen meetings at which I was not present because of the language issues, although I suspect my junior status played a big role in that decision, regardless of the merit of my work. Every idea got rejected, sometimes more than once and often by multiple decision-makers. No-one gave me a reason for the rejections except in one instance where I attended the meeting because the client spoke English. I devised and worked up improvements to a medical device that stretched the body and was designed to alleviate spinal problems. I did, of course, have considerable personal experience of a multitude of medical devices in every kind of environment from NHS hospitals to Northumbria University, where I customised my bedframe so I could do my physiotherapy. The existing device had the appearance of a medieval torture instrument, so I softened its appearance. My logic was impeccable: relaxed patients heal better. It didn't impress the client. After five minutes of silence and head-shaking, he snapped:

– Medical devices just don't look like this!

I countered:

– I agree that your existing medical devices don't look like this but I want to design for the future not the past.

My boss looked at me sternly. I was unsure whether he was offended at the fact that I'd challenged him or at my reasons for doing so. In hindsight, it was probably both. It was also another lesson in how closed the mind can become, bound by what it knows and unable to unleash its imagination with the wonder of a child.

What I experienced in Taiwan and with the toy and luggage companies in the UK is no different to what we have all experienced at some point in every workplace in every town and city in the world. However, when faced with the stifling of our creativity or the silencing of our voice, we have three choices:

Accept it and get on with our job as best as we can.
Go and work elsewhere.
Decide that we can't work for other people and go and set up our own business.

I chose the third option.

Although it was a few years before I'd open the doors of Trunki Towers, I knew that I couldn't live with the frustration of being bound by the judgement of people who based their decisions on short horizons and ingrained habits. If I was going to succeed it would be on my own terms and I knew if I failed I'd accept it was my responsibility and mine alone. That mindset is what every entrepreneur I've ever met has in common. They take risks other people won't take because we value freedom above security. When Littlewoods Pools was little more than a fledgling betting company, it ran into financial difficulty and bankruptcy seemed inevitable. However, despite the bleak outlook, one of the partners, John Moores, offered to buy the other two partners out, even though he struggled to raise the money to do so. Later, he admitted he almost quit himself and credited his wife with changing his mind when she said, 'I'd rather be married to a man who is haunted by failure than one haunted by regret'.

That's the choice we all face: do we choose freedom or security? Do we risk failure on our own terms or risk a life of unlived potential? I'm not criticising anyone who chooses employment over running their own business. All I'm saying is that it's a choice we all have to make and it's important we make it consciously in the full knowledge of what's at stake. Above all, whatever choice we make, it works better when we follow our passion and find our 'element'.

We also need an outlet for our frustrations. Even those of us who choose the relentlessness of running our own business need to lose ourselves at some point. For me, with Kate's death still present and my own life shadowed by CF, I needed space to let go, to stop think-ing. I found that space in warehouse parties and techno dance music. I first started going to techno clubs while I was at university and the dance scene in Taiwan was vibrant and extreme. I spent long nights and hazy mornings dancing, screaming, moving endlessly, chasing away the shadows and sinking my grief in music and movement. The walls that separated my life into necessary segments dissolved and everything flowed with joy and serenity. I shared those moments with friends. In the same way that a combination of solitariness and col-laboration is essential for creative and commercial success, being totally absorbed by movement and music while knowing you are in the company of friends enhances the experience.

Yet I was alone during the rainy season in Taiwan when the roads around my apartment block flooded. Watching objects being swept away, drifting aimlessly, the grey mass of water swallowing the bridge I crossed every day, I lit a lantern in the safety of my seventh floor apartment, opened a can of beer and began modifying sketches for my ride-on suitcase. The sound of the storm and the dim light expanded my horizons; as one life floated away, another flowed towards me. There wasn't much I could do about typhoons; there was a lot I could do about my future. Yes, I thought, I'll take my own path. I owe it to myself. And to Kate.

Hospital
and Hustling

A nother door. Another knock.

The doctor comes in without waiting to be invited. That's the prerogative of the powerful, to come and go as they please.

– How's your coughing been?

I want to answer, then the coughing comes again in gravelly waves, making me retch.

– Not very good then, he says.

Overwhelmed and struck dumb, I look at him like a coughing corpse in an overacted daytime TV drama. I want to say I'm sorry. For the coughing and the drama. But words can't fight their way through gravel. The coughing comes and goes in sharp waves. Outside, the Melbourne sun beats through the windows. It wasn't supposed to be like this. After Taiwan, I'd arrived in Australia with Bec, my girlfriend, to travel along the East Coast starting with the Great Ocean Road. We bought a battered Mazda camper van with a pop-up roof and a blue streak on the side in the hope it lived long enough to make the journey. As it turned out, its life expectancy felt longer than mine after the doctor said to me:

– It's pseudomonas . . .

The sick and wounded have words we like and words we hate. For a cancer patient, *remission* and *palliative* sit neatly on opposite poles of a prognosis, as do *lucky* and *amputation* for a wounded soldier or *thankfully* and *sorry* for those saved the burden of grief or forced to carry it. For me, the best word was *normal* and the worst was *pseudomonas*, the bacteria that destroyed my sister's lungs.

– That explains your coughing.

I want to tell him I know but I can't.

– You'll need to stay here for a while, he goes on, until we've got it under control.

I excavate the word *until*, searching for clues as to which way it's facing, the Great Ocean Road or the undertakers.

When the doctor's gone and I'm alone in the room, the machines around my bed ticking and breathing better than me, I cry, not for me, *never* for me, but for Kate and, in the ugly truth of a hospital washed by antipodean sunlight, for the unfairness of it all. Sometimes that feeling of injustice is too gnawing to control. We all have a compulsion to repeat patterns of behaviour but these are patterns over which we have a measure of control, like toxic relationships that, one after another, have a familiar smell about them or the many paths we take that lead to the same dreary destination. This was different. Knocks on doors and pseudomonas are simply random, repetitive links in a chain that stretches from Kate's death in a hospital in London to my grim bed in Melbourne. How do you deal with that?

I felt my chest rising and falling, rattling, wheezing, mucus blown to pieces by a fit of coughing before reconstituting and the whole process starts over. As I descended into the half-world between wake and sleep, I saw the wall behind which I put my illness. Bits of mortar cracked and flaked, a liquid, sticky like sputum, oozed through. I imagined my hands forcing it back, yelling, *You will not break through. I am not my illness and I will never be my illness*.

Then I slept.

Words came and went, floating inside my mind. They might have been the doctor's or come from other doctors, nurses. I wasn't sure. The words that stuck were mine, repeating like a mantra: 'I can deal with this, I'll get out of here . . . I can deal with this, I'll get out of here . . . I can deal with this, I'll get out of here . . .'

My mind split, out of habit, into problems I could solve and those over which I had no control..

The first step was to shore up the wall. I scoured it for cracks. Those I found, I patched.

I imagined the long, winding path of the Great Ocean Road, the blue sea, a benign sky, barbecues on clifftops, surfing, wrapped up in waves, the curled water rolling around me like a blanket.

After a few days, I felt stronger.

Gradually, *pseudomonas* retreated. The coughing grew calmer. The mucus decreased. The wall held firm.

A nurse said,

– . . .you're over the worst . . . your tests are not indicating pseudo-monus . . . we've got it under control . . .

– Can I have a paper and some pens?

– Of course, the nurse replied, as if it was the strangest request she'd ever been asked.

Over the next few days, as my body got stronger, I forced my mind to focus and my hand to draw.

– What's that? the doctor asked, staring down at sketches for a ride-on suitcase.

– My future, I replied.

I was in hospital, wired up to an IV line for two weeks.

Bec picked me up in the battered Mazda van. On the way back to the flat, as we drove through the streets of Melbourne, brightly coloured parrots flew above us. I'd noticed them when we arrived in the city and now I saw them with new eyes. Living eyes.

– They're beautiful, I said.

– What?

– Nothing.

The day after my discharge, we chugged our way out of Melbourne, heading towards the East Coast. I was still weak from my stay in hospital. I decided to ignore my tiredness. Harsh hospital light gave way to a burning sun, white walls to breathtaking scenery. The world is never more open, more full of possibility, than after a period of confinement. We had little money but it didn't matter. In the mornings, I woke early and walked along clifftops, watching the sunrise. It had never seemed more beautiful or life more precious than it did in the first days of that journey. The vast expanse of nature stretched out before me, yet inside me was a microscopic bacterium, invisible to the naked eye, waiting for its next assault on my life.

I don't drift well nor do I enjoy moving aimlessly. Cosy time travel is reserved for the well, who harbour secret dreams of immortality. They say things like 'Whatever' or 'Mañana' or 'You'll get where you meant to be when the time is right'. They're killing time and I don't have time to kill. I party harder, work harder and focus more intensely than any of my friends. Without CF I might relax and never drive myself to the point of exhaustion but isn't relentlessness the incubator of creativity and success? I've often asked myself if I had the choice would I live a long, complacent life free from major suffering and the answer is always the same: no. If such a life was offered to me I'd decline it or perhaps I just can't conceive of resting before a roaring fire with a full stomach for more than a few days over Christmas.

Now, however, things were different as we drifted along the East Coast, feeling a strange comfort in the idea of being not doing. Almost all of the people we met hung out, made out, surfed, ate, slept, with no purpose other than ease and pleasure. The business of life could wait. Time was on their side and they knew it.

I didn't tell them I spent part of every day refining my designs for Rodeo. Some of the drawings were little more than doodles, others were attempts to dive into some detailed aspect of the product and solve a problem I found there. Usually, I worked on my titanium PowerBook. I'd taught myself computer-aided design (CAD) on this device during my time in Taiwan and I used it to refine my Rodeo designs for manufacture using a computer emulator. I couldn't afford a CAD licence but the free CAD software allowed me to save 25 times before I had to erase everything, reinstall the software and start again. In practice, this meant I had to reinstall the CAD software every few hours. Bec was not alone in thinking I was crazy. To me, it was the only way to pursue my passion so I just got on with it. Wherever I was, in a flat, in hospital, in a camper van, I took tutorials to improve my knowledge of the software. It was tedious but necessary work and this pattern of learning and testing followed me into my business career. Being good at anything means endlessly repeating the same monotonous tasks: success is boring and successful people know it is.

That doesn't mean there's no place for talent. Much of what we are is down to the randomness of genetics and the environments in which we learn. They're the wet nurses of our talent but it's hard work and application that matter most. Without them, we'd never make best use of the gifts, good and bad, that genetics and chance opportunities give us. In my case, I have no doubt that the ambivalent role of horizons in my life, narrow and broad because of the same illness, gave me a focus other people of my age didn't have. The more I laboured at my PowerBook and wrestled with the limitations of learning with unlicensed CAD software, the more certain I became of my purpose and that I was creating a consumer product no-one had thought of before.

I acted like any other young man, fresh out of university. In my mind, however, I knew I was different. Not better or worse. Just different. My relentless, obsessive focus was the mirrored twin of CF: I had them both for the same biological and circumstantial reasons. All I did was play the cards I'd been dealt as best as I was able to. I didn't know or care where the game might take me. I rarely bothered myself with outcomes and acts of God, both equally out of my control. I focused only on what I could do and that was to refine what I create, make it better in any way I could.

After two weeks drifting along the East Coast, I felt re-energised. The surf and sea air cleared my lungs. Life was good but, after taking a few weeks to get to Cairns, the searing heat and humidity played on my chest. That and a lack of cash cut short our journey and we headed back south to Sydney, a city that turned out to be a tale of three jobs, none of which I was any good at.

Initially, I pounded the streets looking for work in a design studio. The contrast with New York was stark. In New York, products were cool. In Sydney, they were black and industrial. Perhaps it was the agencies I happened to visit. In any event, I'd learnt about the stickiness of first impressions at the department of civil engineering at Newcastle University and I struggled to shake off the feeling I was in the wrong place.

When the money ran out, I took a job in a call centre.

– All you have to do, my manager said, is sell the idea that anyone who buys our services will save half the costs of their monthly phone bills. Half! Did you get that? he yelled, pumping his fists.

– Yes, the team shouted.

I couldn't even say 'Yes' in my mind. The whole situation felt ridiculous.

I was given a booth, close to my friend Jared who'd introduced me to the job. He was a web designer and, like many people in the call centre, was treading water, looking for a way out.

I wanted to ask if anyone would mind if I did some CAD drawings between calls. Instead, I got on with the job. My manager gave me a book with lots of phone numbers in it, together with an instruction to 'call and close' as many deals as I could. Some people in the office did well. There was a group of callers near me who made quite a bit of money by ignoring the lists they'd been given and calling their own network.

I didn't have a network and I was predictably useless. I didn't make a single sale and the inevitable bullet came after two weeks.

Desperate for money, I was told about a job selling CHUBB security systems door to door. This time I went one better and made a sale to a man who'd recently emigrated from Johannesburg to Sydney. I didn't have to work hard to get the deal. The man sold it to himself.

– Where I come from, he said, there's so much crime. We're always scared and here's no different.

In fact, Sydney *was* different. It was many times safer than Johannesburg. The fact that the man conflated the two cities into one experience is just another example of how negative experiences imprint themselves on our minds more firmly than positive ones. Still, I was grateful for my only sale. The rest of the time, I faced rejections without having the will or ingenuity to talk my way through them.

Selling is a problem like any other. I faced prospects who were not expecting me, who had no idea what I was selling, who didn't think they wanted what I was selling and it was my job to create sufficient urgency until they realised they needed an alarm system *now*! My failure to solve this problem wasn't down to my selling skills. I sell myself and my design ideas very well. This problem was different in the most important aspect of all: other than the fact that I needed money, I didn't care about what I was selling. Every time I picked up the phone or knocked on a door, I felt I was about to take something from someone, force them into giving me something, regardless of whether it was in their interest or not. Rationally, saving money on phone bills or putting an alarm system on the front of your house is a good thing, but that misses the point. Often, selling, with its targets and prizes, becomes an end in itself and what motivates people is the thrill of the chase, the close, the seduction. From politics to law, speed dating to winning friends and influencing people, it's the person with the most charisma, a memorable phrase or a powerful disposition, who wins the day, not the person with the strongest case who actually believes in what they're doing. We're a species of senseless seducers, moving from one seduction to the next, deepening our narcissism with every deal we close.

In business terms, this was an important lesson for me to learn. You can have the best product and the best service team to support it but, if you can't sell, then a worse product and a worse service team will steal your market. They may lose it in the long term, but unless you can make your business work in the short term, there's no long term to worry about.

Despite this, for me, building a sustainable business means having a passion for what I do. In practical terms, this means caring about what I sell, how I sell it and who I sell it to. Business, in this sense, is about giving not taking and perhaps that's why my third job in Australia was more suited to my disposition.

AMEX took me on in their customer service department and I revelled in the role of helping people solve problems they knew they had as opposed to selling them products they didn't want. The calls I took were bland in terms of the problems I was asked to solve. I took abuse from people who felt they'd been let down by AMEX. I learned quickly that, even though I was an inconsequential cog in this enormous corporate machine, to the people on the other end of the phone, I might as well have been the founder and main shareholder. Years later, as the owner of my own business, I remembered those dissatisfied customers, furious because of preventable problems, and it fed into my determination to put customer engagement at the heart of my brand. Psychologists have shown that we recall bad experiences more readily than good ones and one unhappy customer will undo the commercial benefits of 10 happy ones.

Between calls or when the disgruntled masses took a break from their moral crusade, I worked on designs for Rodeo. The call-sheets got covered in doodles, designs for catch mechanisms, wheel hub solutions and an endless array of horn fixing options.

So, when I left Australia and returned to the UK, I came back armed with a simple rule about how I'd conduct my business life: I'll squeeze every drop of life out of every day I have, I'll live knowing there's no end to the problems I can solve and I'll only sell what I believe in.

Of course, those are fine ideals but I was jobless and penniless, so I signed on at the Job Centre.

– What career are you looking for? a man in a loose fitting check jacket and rolled up shirt sleeves, asked me in my interview.

– I'm going to run my own business.

– I see, he said, looking up at me. Do you have any money?

– No.

– I see.

The conversation ended with him recommending a number of courses about starting your own business. I thanked him and went straight back to hustling for work. Unlike my incompetence in selling cheap phone bills and alarm systems, I was very good at selling myself to design consultancies. Despite being based in Chester, I made a list of top London design consultancies. Every call started in the same way:

– Hello, my name's Rob Law. I've got a first class degree from Northumbria University, I've won a design award for a consumer product and I'm working near your office next week (Note: I was never working near anybody's office because I was stuck at home) so I was wondering if I could pop in and introduce myself.

Most calls need an appointment and, in trying to make one, I proved to myself that I was good and bad at selling: good when I valued what I was selling and bad when I didn't. Generally, the meetings went well. No-one ever threw me out and I was offered a number of opportunities. I took one at Tangerine. I felt like a stalker. As well as preceding me at Northumbria University, Jonathan Ive was one of the founders of this consultancy before he moved to Apple. I'm like anyone else, a compulsive pattern-maker, finding connections in events that are as unrelated as economic predictions and the movement of markets, so I convinced myself that a completely random coincidence was, in fact, a good omen.

Tangerine was everything I expected it to be. Creative, dynamic and ruthless, I loved being among product designers pushing each other to create ever more inventive products. The consultancy was responsible for the first British Airways flat bed and I worked on mobile phones for Samsung, air conditioning units for LG and luxury beds for major retail brands.

I spent every spare moment outside work refining Rodeo for manufacture, working out the basics of what I needed to run a successful business and focusing, with greater ferocity than ever, on the problems I had to solve to make that dream a reality. When the work dried up, I retreated back home to Chester. Kate's room was unchanged and the moment I walked through the front door, I became the boy who never left, stuck in a cage gilded with love and memories. Today, the world is full of boomerang kids who come back home and never leave. I understand the seduction, the battered slippers they fall into only to find they can never take them off. I knew if I didn't leave, Kate's room would become mine and I had a promise to keep. So, I lived on air and love, mindful to leave sufficient space to build a road back to the city. I worked obsessively, refining designs for Rodeo, planning the business I wanted to run.

I approached the Prince's Trust for a grant to set up my own business. They taught me how to write a business plan, complete with financial projections. I understood that, in the short term I'd need to earn a living as a freelance product designer. In the business plan I wrote:

> In order to succeed in this market I intend to sell my skills cheaply to get a foot in the door and develop a client relationship. Once this has been established my rate and volume of work will increase. . .My direct competition comes from other freelance designers who may have more experience than myself. However, with my lower rates, international experience and achievements, I hope to present a very attractive service to design consultancies.

Instinctively, I felt I had to demonstrate two things to the Prince's Trust: capability and humility. The last thing I wanted to do was 'sell my skills cheaply' but I understood what retailers call a 'loss leader': if I took a financial hit in the short term, I had sufficient belief in Rodeo and my product design capabilities to know I'd gain in the medium term.

From all the hustling I'd done, I'd picked up a valuable business lesson: when you sell yourself or any products and services you supply into any market, never allow vanity to dictate your pricing strategy. If you let your ego drive your price, you'll end up blaming everyone except yourself for the failures that follow. You'll do this because your ego has to preserve its infallibility at any cost. You'll repeat the same pattern again and again; failure will mount upon failure, until you either learn to demote your ego in your business decision-making or you end up in prison, which is the inevitable consequence of spinning your judgement in a spiral of self-delusion.

My business plan was further complicated by the fact that Rodeo was a novel product, 'a hybrid of a ride-on toy and a suitcase and therefore creates a niche in the market'. In the plan, knowing I had to opt for luggage or toy, I positioned the product as a toy. However, all I knew for certain was that it solved two problems: distraction for bored kids and respite for harassed parents.

Finally, my first ever business plan provided financial projections on sales and cash, which never materialised. I've yet to produce a plan that matched expectations and the best advice I can give any business is that your business plan is a direction of travel not a blueprint to be followed rigidly. The moment after you've bound your plan and sent it to your accountant, your bankers and your fellow directors, it will have changed beyond recognition.

Failure to acknowledge these real-world effects on planning and goal-setting sets up what Professor Chris Kayes calls 'goalodicy', which he describes as

> the more a person, group or organisation relies on a future as yet unachieved goal as a source of identity, the more likely they will persist at pursuing the goal beyond what is reasonable. . .Ultimately the goal becomes the primary identity of the goal setter and abandoning the goal becomes as unthinkable as abandoning oneself.

Of course, I've set goals and when Rodeo became Trunki, it had the single-minded goal of being 'the global travel brand for families'. The difference is, I've never anchored my identity or my business to any single objective, even the ones closest to my heart. Success depends on flexibility and, where any personal or business objective starts to corrode your ability to adapt to changing circumstances on the ground, abandon it. If you don't, then prepare to sink into oblivion along with your goals.

I was awarded a £4,000 loan from the Prince's Trust and a £500 grant. More important than the money was the mentor, Philip, who came with the award. For the first time in my life I had money and professional guidance. I never knew much about him other than that he was a successful entrepreneur. Of the many things he did, three had a big impact on my life: he taught me that businesses run on cash, that decision-makers have limited attention spans and therefore elevator pitches are effective selling tools. Four years later, long after our formal engagement had stopped, he emailed me the name of a researcher at the BBC. 'Have you thought of going on Dragons' Den', he wrote, 'and here's the person you need to talk to.'

Philip also encouraged me to visit more manufacturers so in February 2003 I went to a toy fair at ExCel in London. Armed with an A4 folder showcasing pictures of Rodeo together with samples from my business plan, I worked out my target companies. I avoided the big companies because they wouldn't be interested in taking a speculative product by an unknown designer. I also avoided the smaller companies as they'd be unable to take on the licensing and manufacture of the product.

There were about a dozen companies left on my list. I mapped my route around the show. The first three companies thanked me for my brief presentation and concluded with a variation of 'We're not

exactly sure what you've got here. We think there might be something in it but it's not for us.'

Then came the fourth stand. Having hustled around London, New
York and Sydney looking for design work, nothing phased me. I knew
it was a numbers game and the key to success was forgetting about
every knock back the instant after it happened. It's a cliché to talk
about the resilience of successful entrepreneurs but that doesn't
make it any less true. There's a mindset you have to have that's
based on three basic behaviours:

Never feed off past success or wallow in past failures. Either of
these attitudes is an indulgence neither you nor your business
can afford.

Treat every prospect with dignity and respect. It may be your
10th meeting of the day but, for your prospect, it's their first.
If you're exhausted, act fresh. If you're hungry, act like you've
just eaten. If you're losing your confidence, act confident and
no-one will know the difference.

Keep going. Keep going. Keep going . . .

My presentation to the fourth company, Toyline International, went
as predictably as the others in every aspect except their response:

– This is the best product we've seen in a long time. You've got a deal.

Within two months, in March 2003, I'd signed a 'Technology Transfer Agreement' giving me a 5% royalty on all sales. While Toyline
loved the name Rodeo, a quick investigation brought up a number
of trademark issues. We brainstormed some alternatives and settled on Trunki because the front of the ride-on suitcase, with its tow
strap for kids to grip, looked like the trunk of an elephant. I liked it.
It was memorable, paid homage to early luggage trunks and easy to
trademark.

After the agreement was signed I was euphoric. I was 22 and I'd done my first significant business deal. That euphoria, while understandable, was also my undoing. I projected a seamless line of successes stretching into the indefinite future. I've never been motivated by money but I felt blessed that my future was secure being paid for what I loved doing. Above all, I thought of Kate. I was living a life for both of us.

Tooling and manufacturing were set up in China and they'd ship containers loaded with Trunkis from Hong Kong to large retailers anywhere in various parts of the world. In the summer, I finalised the CAD drawings ready for manufacture, sat back and waited for the royalties to flood in.

In the hiatus between design and manufacture, I wanted to keep on learning so I took a position as a junior designer at Kinneir Dufort in Bristol. The company was established and successful and they asked me to solve a number of consumer and medical product problems. In May 2004, the first major order of 3,288 Trunkis was shipped to the Middle East. It felt like I was riding an unstoppable wave, except this wave, like all waves, crashed into nothing.

A month after the Trunkis were dispatched, Toyline called me.

– We're struggling, Rob.

– What with?

– Everything.

– Can you be more specific?

– Sales are way behind forecast, manufacturing is challenging and we can't pay your royalties.

– That sounds pretty much like everything!

We ended the call amicably. He suggested I buy half the tooling for US$15,000 plus the royalties I was owed. I'd then take increased royalty payments as part of the deal. I asked for 12.5%. We settled on 8.75%.

When I looked at what they'd been doing, I realised the basic mistake they'd made. They'd pitched Trunki as a ride-on toy without any reference to the fact that it was also a piece of luggage. The pervasive effect of ingrained habits on people's commercial vision had struck again. I looked at a TV ad a retailer had produced and it was all about kids riding around on a Trunki inside the house. Not an airport in sight. The problem this approach caused should have been obvious. Toy retailers already had a glut of ride-on toys and Trunki was more expensive than all of them. How, then, could they hope to sell a product in a saturated market to over-fed consumers? Except, the market for Trunki wasn't saturated. It was new but it takes vision and a healthy attitude to risk to imagine new markets and that was proving the biggest challenge of all. So I decided to solve it as best as I could.

I locked myself away and created a presentation explaining what a Trunki was. I focused on family travel and backed up my presentation with online research undertaken by Mintel on the travel market. I presented branding associations with travel companies like Virgin and Butlins together with nine Trunki variations, ranging from cats to zebras.

– I'm sorry, Rob, the MD of Toyline said, We're in the toy business not the luggage business.

In October 2005, I took a phone call. The MD called again to say Toyline was going into voluntary liquidation. In the 18 months they'd represented Trunki, they'd sold 14,556 units and I'd earned $9,675 in royalties, half of which was still owed.

When your dream breaks, what do you do next?

The first thing is to know, before you even start dreaming, that *every* dream breaks in the end. What stops us from seeing this is a hard-wired optimism bias. This bias serves us well when times are bad but when times are good it lowers our defences and blinds us to the truth that time isn't tame, that the future will not bend to our will. This truth is what makes a book like *The Secret* so harmful. Nurtured in a pre-crunch world of easy credit and subprime lending, it sold the absurd fantasy that the universe bends to our will if only we know how to ask. The author, Rhonda Byrne, claims that 'you deserve all the good things in life' and 'thoughts become things'. Translated into human psychology, this means that if you think about some-thing you'll get it because you're a good person who's owed it by the universe. This staggering exercise in narcissistic self-delusion was propped up by sub-prime mortgage lending and the endlessly inven-tive ways in which bankers and brokers built their fortunes on sand.

Failure is inevitable and universal and we forget this truth at our peril. Excessive optimism breeds a feeling of invincibility that feeds the delusions of our ego. However large or small your dreams, the big-gest protection you need is against yourself. You simply can't afford to take anything for granted in life or in business. Especially success.

After the call about winding up Toyline, I was in shock for about five minutes, then I got back to work, planning how I could take Trunki to market as what I'd always known it was: not a toy, not a piece of lug-gage but a consumer life-style brand.

I understood what the product was.

Kids understood what the product was.

The only people who seemed unable to grasp it were those responsible for manufacturing and selling it.

The only solution, therefore, was to do it myself.

I went out for a run, the familiar pounding of my shoes on the road beating my future into shape.

Before Christmas 2005, less than two months after I'd been told my dream was over and Toyline was winding up, I placed a purchase order with the factory in China for 1,400 Trunkis before spending a family holiday in Canada working on branding, a revised business plan and a new website which Jared, free at last from the call centre, was building for me. I was skint. I'd spent my savings on the trip to Australia and the royalties paid for a mountain bike and that was it. I applied for a £10,000 personal loan. My gran lent me £2,000. I was back in business. In January 2007, as soon as I got back from Canada, I bought the Trunki trademark from the Toyline administrator for £300 and an old friend from university designed the logo.

I was set to go. I was in control. The branding and positioning of the product were right. The market was right. What could possibly go wrong this time?

The answer: everything.

At the end of January, the factory in China went bust.

The only bit of good news was that I hadn't handed over any money. I set about finding a new manufacturing plant through an agent in Hong Kong. It took less than a month.

In April 2006, MoCoLoCo.com, my favourite contemporary design blog, featured Trunki, positioning it as 'the world's first ever ride-on suitcase for globetrotting kids'. The response was as overwhelming as it was unpredictable. Emails and enquiries flooded in from the USA, Australia, Asia, from all over the world. One was from the Museum of Modern Art in New York. They ordered 650 units. Orders poured in from online and offline catalogues as interest in Trunki grew beyond anything I expected and, on 5 May 2006, I crossed the commercial Rubicon: 1,400 Terrance and Trixie Trunki arrived at Avonmouth Docks. I quit my design job.

Then I hit a problem: angry customers. Parents said that when their child sat on the Trunki, the catches popped open. I ran a check at the warehouse. They were right. It happened on about 10% of Trunkis. In the rush to start production, a metal hinge was formed 2mm short and I learned that 2mm is the vast distance that separates a happy customer from an unhappy one.

I acted quickly and contacted customers, apologising that their Trunki had caught a cold on the high seas and arrived in the UK with a dose of the Trunki sneezes. They seemed to enjoy their first experience of Trunki humour. We received many letters of thanks when we remade the hinges to the correct dimensions and sent them out with a simple instruction sheet called The Sniffles Remedy, a step-by-step guide to replacing the catches.

That still left another problem unsolved. There were 1,350 Trunkis in stock and they all had to have the catches replaced. I press-ganged friends and family, including a cousin visiting from Canada, to open every box, remove the wrapping, open the Trunki, unscrew the old hinge, replace it with the new one, test it and repackage it. We got the process down to five minutes per Trunki and, within two weeks, I was back in control. All I needed now was the funding and mentoring to make the business work.

And that's when the email from Philip, my mentor at the Prince's Trust, came in suggesting I go on Dragons' Den.

I didn't hesitate.

I emailed the researcher at the BBC, with the header, *Dragons Ride-on Trunki*.

The biggest lesson of my life was about to be delivered.

Dragons and Strap Hooks

T he judgement of even the most powerful people is easily over-whelmed by simple things . . . . . . like strap hooks . . .

The evening before the biggest failure in the history of Dragons' Den, I sat down to dinner and a final run through with my father.

– That's great, Rob, he said. You feel OK?

– Can we go through the financials one more time?

We ended up going through it twice. I got the numbers into my head: three-year growth forecasts, cash flow projections, profit forecasts.

This, I thought to myself, is what Dragons want. Figures tame them. Like all successful entrepreneurs, they're risk-takers but they're also rational decision-makers. All I've got to do is convince them of the commercial viability of a ride-on suitcase on their terms: financials first. My terms might have been on the lived experience of using a Trunki, the fun it would bring to kids and their parents and, above all, the brand itself. But, in the Den, figures put out fires.

After finishing the second run through I was good to go.

When I got up the following morning, I stood in the window of my hotel and looked out. The sky sat grey and heavy over London. Despite the drab landscape, I felt good, reassured by the hum of traffic. I repeated the elevator pitch like a mantra.

About an hour later, Dad met me in the lobby and we began our walk to the Den. We didn't say much on the short walk to London Bridge. My chest felt tight and I needed to get some of the mucus off my lungs. For months, I'd been working harder than I'd ever worked before. I'd start in the early morning and finish in the early hours of the following morning. It took a serious toll on my health. There were days when I forgot to take my medication or skipped my physiotherapy. My lungs protested but I couldn't, or wouldn't, stop.

I'm lacking in emotional introspection, so the most useful insights about my life haven't come from me, they've come from friends, colleagues, my business coach. What I've always known with absolute certainty is that my focus was, and is, on the present. The one challenge that drives everything I do is solving problems and finding solutions or finding a new set of problems I didn't know existed. It anchors me firmly in the moment and acts as a bulwark against the temptation towards melancholy. That kind of immersive behaviour and the hard work that makes it possible are essential to success. Focus and repetition are necessary to be good at anything from product design to composing symphonies. 'Anyone who works as hard as me,' said the composer J.S. Bach, 'will compose music that is just as good.'

As for the CF, I was indifferent to its course or in denial with regard to its existence. Either way, it was a pretence. Anyone who suffers from a major illness knows that indifference and denial never last long. Any illness will make its presence felt and mine was no different. As we walked, I coughed violently, paving the road with mucus. *Follow the yellow brick road, follow the yellow brick road . . .*

Slung over my shoulder, Terrance and Trixie looked relaxed and confident. It's just another problem to solve, I told myself as I ran over the presentation in my head. We turned down a street and came face to face with a large warehouse. Against the grey sky it looked imposing, a brooding lair dropped from Middle Earth into East London. I felt my stomach turn with excitement.

Inside was as industrial as I expected. Crumbling walls, exposed brick, a dimly lit cave haunted by iron and steel ghosts that once clanked and clamoured down its narrow passageways. Evan Davis, the presenter, and two researchers greeted us. Everyone smiled. I smiled back. Busy and professional, they moved like gothic gatekeepers whose job it is to keep guests from fleeing before being fed to the Dragons.

Mucus rattled in my chest. I wanted to cough.

I looked around for monitors. There weren't any. A wooden staircase loomed in the distance. The more observant of the gatekeepers saw me looking at it and ushered me into the Green Room. It was dark grey not green. I asked when I'd be called to the Den. She said she didn't know. It could be anytime. Unlike Theseus on his mazy path to meet the Minotaur, I didn't even have a ball of string to give me a means of escape. I was at the mercy of the Den and its creatures. I looked around at the other contestants. We smiled at each other without speaking; knights before battle we prepared our attack and rehearsed our defence in silence.

A young man with a clipboard and headphones told me I was third into the Den. Having a number, a place in the order of things, gave me a feeling of control. A short while later, he came back into the dark grey room and asked if I was ready. I said yes. It was either that or going home in disgrace. I followed him to the spiral staircase, apologising to Terrance and Trixie for holding them too tightly. As

I climbed the staircase to where the Dragons waited, I felt relaxed. I knew my pitch. I knew the numbers. Above all, I knew I had a great product and a powerful brand and I knew what I wanted: £100,000 for 10% of the business.

I reached the top of the staircase. Five Dragons faced me. The battle was on.

Whenever I pitch a product, I keep the process as structured as I can and I know, if I'm going to close a deal, I've got to keep the messages simple. The Prince's Trust taught me that. There are also good evolutionary reasons for this: our brains evolved to process very little information at any given time and to make quick decisions. If you're going to close a deal, avoid complexity at all costs and stay in control of the pitch at all times. In the Den, I failed on both counts.

It began well.

I'd rehearsed my elevator pitch, compete with choreography (I made a point of sitting on Terrance) and I delivered it perfectly:

– Meet Terrance and Trixie, the world's first and only ride-on suitcase for globetrotting tots. Toddlers can pack, sit on and ride their Trunki while parents can keep their kids in tow, quite literally, with the child sitting on the case. Trunkis are lightweight and durable and made of the same materials as adult suitcases. To date we've sold 20,000 units . . . Thank you for your time and would anyone like to test ride a Trunki.

Richard Farleigh volunteered. I was pleased it was him as he was the Dragon I wanted as an investor. I'd researched each Dragon, their behaviours, strengths and weaknesses, and I knew Richard had two small children. As I towed him around the studio, I joked his kids would still need a Trunki even on a private jet. He then towed me. Deborah Meaden got up, took Trixie for a walk and came back saying

Trunkis were very obedient and, despite having fixed wheels, Trixie managed to turn and keep close to her heels. Everything was going perfectly. When the test drives finished, I noticed Theo Paphitis holding Trixie, tugging hard at the strap.

Later, he said:

– When the Trunki first came in. I thought it was quite cute.

So did Deborah:

– I loved it. I thought it was a really cute product. I could see why kids would enjoy riding on it. Then Theo got hold of it . . .

And that changed everything.

It was the hardest I'd ever seen anyone tug at the strap. He wore his constipation face as he pulled harder. Why was he pulling so hard? What was he doing to Trixie? A bead of sweat dripped off his forehead. I watched in disbelief, waiting for fire to shoot from his nostrils. The other Dragons stared at him. Then it happened. A click, noiseless, like watching the shifting of tectonic plates from inside a vacuum. The strap popped. There was a moment's silence. The Dragons turned to face me.

– Is this a faulty catch? Theo asked, holding the wound he'd inflicted on Trixie in his hand.

– No, it's not, I replied. You've pulled the hook off there, yeah.

I'd lost control in my use of the word 'yeah' as I leaned nervously towards him. I felt sweat on my palms. Without a lance, a magic potion or Gandalf, I knew I was in trouble.

– I shouldn't have been able to pull the strap off, though, should I? he said.

I had no idea what to say. This is one eventuality I hadn't prepared for.

– These hooks are rubbish, he said, waving the broken strap at me.

– I didn't design that, I said.

– But they are rubbish.

– Yeah.

That word again. Clumsy. Scented with defeat. I was lost.

– You've got problems with the product, he said, after Deborah Madden declared herself out.

– Problems that can be solved, I interrupted, unable to understand how I'd lost control and why such a small, easily solved design problem had been magnified out of all proportion to its actual significance.

– But you shouldn't come here with problems, he snapped back, without identifying them or sorting them out first. It drives me mad that we actually waste our time with these things. I, too, am out.

If I'd had any doubt whether his anger was real or whether he was playing to the cameras, that doubt vanished: he was seriously pissed off!

Peter Jones was the next to attack:

– This product isn't patentable and within seven days I could do a better job than that, make sure the clips are working and I could have this in production by the end of next month. Your company is currently worthless. I'm out.

That left Richard Farleigh, my main target. Seeing an opportunity to get a product whose potential he, alone, could see, he pounced. He offered £100,000 for half the company. I turned him down. I'd have given him 20% but he was in no mood for negotiation. Dragons are intemperate creatures.

Duncan Bannatyne was last to declare himself out.

– I wouldn't buy it. I wouldn't invest in the company so I've no interest in the product at all so I'm going to declare myself out.

Then the Dragons began mocking the product.

– We'll call it a Dunki, quipped Peter Jones, imagining a name for the product he said he'd have in the shelves within a month.

Everyone laughed.

When the laughter stopped, the Dragons thanked me, politely, for my efforts. In a last gesture of defiance, I offered Terrance and Trixie to Richard, two for the price of one. He accepted. A few weeks later I received a Coutts cheque for £25 posted from Monaco. Looking back, I wished I'd framed it but after leaving the Den empty-handed, cash was tight.

As I walked back down the stairs, the clank of my steps echoing through the Den, a roar of laughter followed me.

I was in shock.

It felt like everything I'd worked for had collapsed.

I think I spoke to Evan Davis downstairs.

I saw my Dad. He hadn't heard or seen what happened.

I said a few words then we left.

– Was it that bad? Dad asked on the way back to the hotel.

– Yes, I said.

– You'll be alright, he said. You've fought back from worse than this.

Shock is a signal that the world has changed but we're not sure exactly how it's changed or what the implications will be. All we know is something significant has happened and that's how I felt.

Later that evening, the shock subsided and that's when the catastrophising began. It went like this:

I'm going to be on TV.

Trunki broke.

The world will witness my failure.

Trunki is finished.

I'm finished.

Everything's over.

In the studio, I'd felt completely out of control. Now I was rationalising the real-life effects of that failure and, in that moment, they felt insurmountable. I wished I'd never ventured into the Den and I wished I'd invented a time machine not a Trunki.

Every life and every business has moments like this, when our plans fail and we lose the balance of our mind, where a failure of one thing leads, in our frantic imagination, to the failure of everything. This is what is meant by 'catastrophising' when we spend hours, days, weeks, years even, worrying about things that never happen. In the real world, as opposed to the fantasies we play in our minds, things rarely, if ever, turn out as badly as we fear and, if they do, we find we have resources we never knew we had that enable us to cope with them. What matters when you face those moments of fear, anxiety and self-doubt, is that you do two things:

Breathe deeply and slowly.

Stop thinking.

So that's what I did. I told myself it was just another problem to solve. I may have felt with absolute certainty backed by a mountain of evidence that there wasn't a solution, but I knew there was one. I just hadn't found it yet.

That thought helped. For a short while.

Later that night, staring across the city from my hotel room, I felt a searing pain in my chest and my lungs clogged up.

When did I last take my medication or do my physiotherapy?

I wasn't sure.

I thought of Kate, briefly. I couldn't afford to dwell too long in that place in case the wall began to crumble. The illness had to stay behind it. If it ever got out, then . . .

I went over what happened and, from nowhere, I whispered,

– Burden's Baby . . .

I was back in school, bullying voices taunting me.

I wiped a hand across my brow and closed my eyes. I hated what I saw. I've never felt like a victim or behaved like one. Whatever life has thrown at me, I've dealt with as best as I can, without complaint or recrimination. There was just something about the way the Dragons behaved that brought all this shit up. I know they hadn't intended it or had any conscious awareness of their behaviour but they'd behaved like a pack and I was the prey.

How had Theo have gone from 'cute product' and Deborah from 'I loved it' to dismissing Trunkis out of hand because of a popped strap hook and then rounding on me, laughing, mocking.

Theo Paphitis began the frenzy. Speaking later, he said,

– If anyone was tempted to invest in Trunki, when the strap came off, I think people thought 'Nah, not for us'.

As with all frenzies, this was one was contagious and Deborah Meaden was next to be bitten:

– The moment Theo pulled that handle off, the whole integrity of the quality of that product was compromised.

This was the first mistake the Dragons made. It's an easy one to make. We've all done it at some point, when we let a small detail, with strong emotional impact, overwhelm our capacity to reason. Psychologists call it the availability bias. It's what happens when one piece of information is so much more cognitively accessible that it negates everything else. The result is impaired or biased decision-making. In this case, the theatricality of Theo's performance prejudiced the perspective of the group. I remember when I was at school, learning about the War of Jenkins' Ear, when the severed ear of an eighteenth-century British naval captain, Robert Jenkins, was produced in Parliament. This public display became decisive in Britain declaring war on Spain. Something similar happened in the lead up to the second Iraq War in 2003, when US Secretary of State Colin Powell produced two aluminium tubes he claimed Saddam Hussein purchased for his covert nuclear weapons programme. Like Jenkins' ear, the tubes moved hearts and changed minds. That they were empty of anything other than deceit was lost in the fog of war.

In every area of our life, we have to remain vigilant, otherwise one or more of the many cognitive biases, hard-wired into the architecture of our brains, will infect the decisions we make. Trunki was just as cute, lovable and commercially viable after the strap hook popped as it was before. All that changed was the capacity of the Dragons to see the potential of the product stood before them. That is the price we all pay for letting prejudice dominate our thinking.

The other effect of Theo's performance was to turn four of the five Dragons (Richard Farleigh being the exception) into a pack. When Theo struck, they sensed blood and attacked. It reminded me of a documentary I watched about Jane Goodall and her discovery of the nature of chimpanzee aggression. In the mid-1970s, she recorded details of what became known as the Gombe Chimpanzee War between two rival troops. The fighting was relentless and coordinated, as one troop, the Kasekela, raided the territory of a neighbouring troop, the Kahama. One of the notable features of the raids was the tendency of the Kasekela chimps to attack isolated chimps from the Kahama and butcher them. Cyril Grueter, a primate researcher at the University of Western Australia, reviewed Goodall's work and concluded that 'the costs of attacking a single chimpanzee are often negligible, thus promoting escalation of conflict'.

This is exactly what happened in the Den. Outnumbered, four Dragons against one man and two Trunkis, Theo Paphitis started an assault that the other Dragons escalated. Everyone lost their judgement, including me.

My defence when Theo attacked the broken strap hook was pathetic. 'I didn't design it' isn't a defence. It's an abdication of responsibility. I was like the business owner who absolves himself for a poor outcome by saying one of his managers made the key decision, forgetting or refusing to accept that he employed the manager and is, ultimately, accountable for every decision the business makes. I have never ducked responsibility like that before or since and I later ensured that I designed every part of a Trunki. However, it didn't matter whether I designed the strap hook or not. I owned the business so it was entirely my responsibility. That kind of misjudgement happens in the heat of battle, as I'm sure many chimps of the Kahama troop discovered to their cost.

What surprised me more, in hindsight, about the behaviour of the Dragons, was their inability to see the power of a branded product. Peter Jones wrote off Trunki because it wasn't patentable. Other Dragons nodded in agreement. However, the lack of a patent doesn't in any way affect the success of a product if it builds a strong brand in the consumer's mind. From my own experience of taking a wide variety of pharmaceutical drugs, I convinced myself that Nurofen was a better product than ibuprofen, even though they're identical. Again, that's the power of branding. Perfumes provide a countless number of examples of non-patentable products that thrive because of effective branding. In fact, it's much easier to copy a product than it is to replicate a brand. Once a brand is established in a given market, it can be very difficult to dislodge.

What, then, makes a great brand? It's good but not essential if a product is unique or easy to differentiate. Trunki ticked that box as there was no product anywhere in the world that did what Trunki did. That's why toy manufacturers and luggage manufacturers struggled to understand how to position it. What matters most in branding is how the product is positioned and marketed. Despite the inability of retailers and manufacturers to break their habits of thinking, Trunki was immediately understood by kids and parents, the primary target market, and that was its strength.

'A brand,' wrote former Disney CEO Michael Eisner, 'is a living entity and it is enriched or undermined cumulatively over time, the product of a thousand small gestures.' Those gestures are how a brand behaves and range from how a representative of a brand answers the telephone to the brand logo and the common features of a product range. It's about building a world around your brand that consumers like and understand. In my case, The Sniffles Remedy made parents smile when Catch Replacement Instructions would have made them snarl.

In the digital age, a brand is also what consumers decide it is. The era of brand control is over, as brands evolve through consumer engagement as much as boardroom intent and generating that engagement is the role of marketing. For me, that engagement had always been important and became critical after I emerged from the Den. I think of marketing and branding like a mating ritual. In the same way as a peacock's tail or the bower of a bowerbird is a mating signal designed to guarantee the transmission of genetic material from one generation to the next, then a brand is the means by which products and services ensure their transmission from one generation of consumers to the next. And in both cases, the mechanics of that transmission is the same: attraction.

Brands act as ornaments or fitness indictors that tell the world who we are and what we stand for. They don't just sell products; they have values which they articulate through advertising, sponsorship, affiliations with sports stars and the design of their stores. The goal of marketing is replication and, as such, the arms race of brands is structured in the same way as any competition for mates. It's a game of winner takes all and the marketing methods brands use to attract consumers will become more inventive and costly over time as they battle to increase their market share. Superbrands are simply a natural consequence of this evolution. When the French newspaper *La Presse* became the first to allow advertising on its pages in 1836, the ads were simple and cheap but, in 2008, Guinness spent over £10 million on a single television advert, which was a model of waste in the service of propagation. More than 6,000 dominoes, 10,000 books, 4,000 tyres, 75 mirrors, 50 fridges, 45 wardrobes and six cars were destroyed in the making of a single commercial.

In the world of brands, a small number of companies have evolved into superbrands. Their commercial DNA has proved so successful they are now capable of displays of almost unimaginable cost. The challenge superbrands make to their competitors is match us or die and perhaps the ultimate superbrand is Apple. The story of Apple is the story of escalating displays of technological innovation. The company consistently cannibalises its own innovations and bundles them in an evolving range of new and better products. For instance, the revolutionary iPod was bundled as an app when the iPhone was launched. But products were only a part of what turned Apple from a business into a superbrand. What mattered was how it placed these products in a narrative of freedom and gratuitous display within a messianic framework. An iMac, MacBook, iPhone, iPod or iPad are simply machines designed to organise and transfer information. But for us to consume them with fervour and to do so repeatedly, so that we become their means of replication, demands that they become so much more than that. The wasteful displays of power from the 1984 launch commercial through to extravagant packaging and cathedral-like stores are what turn buyers into believers, just as the quality of a mating display turns a casual observer into a sexual partner.

In any activity where propagation is the goal, then selection will be the means to achieve it and it will always involve displays whose cost escalates as the demand for cheap copies pushes the need for authenticity to new heights of innovation. 'Innovation,' said Steve Jobs, 'distinguishes between a leader and a follower.' Staying ahead of the competition means developing new techniques of seduction and any method of selection followed by many will always become gradually less successful over time as it is overtaken by the few who know how to innovate.

These rules apply to every business, large or small. You may not be able to spend millions on an advertising campaign or have an equivalent of Googleplex as your Head Office but you can put customer engagement and innovation at the heart of what you do. That's why Trunki is on its fifth version and there will be many more to come as details are refined on the basis of customer feedback. For example, Trunki MK2 evolved to solve a problem some parents had. As one father put it: 'I know Trunkis are designed for kids but please put some bloody handles on it so I can carry it up an escalator without collapsing!' I did. Trunki MK2 also saw the introduction of 'teddy bear seatbelts' and secret compartments for kids to hide their sweets.

Innovating with new products became central to making Trunki a global brand. While packing a dry bag during a camping trip I noticed, when I held it horizontally, that it looked like a catfish. That moment was the inspiration behind Paddelpak, a series of eight waterproof backpacks for kids to take swimming, each one named after a sea character from clown fish to sharks. Another travel innovation was ToddlePak, a children's harness inspired by an ultra-marathon backpack I saw at an outdoor sports exhibition in Germany. The backpack had a pull cord to ensure a perfect fit. I adapted that idea and the result was a harness that adjusted to fit the child. As with every Trunki product, each harness was a colourful character and, despite being four times the price of competitor products, it became a best-seller in the UK and China.

If you stop innovating, your business will fail and when Apple was in crisis, failing to attract sufficient customers, Jobs knew the answer: 'The cure for Apple is not cost cutting. The cure for Apple is to innovate its way out of its current predicament.' Selection is never about spending less; it's about becoming more. The only way to become more is to take risks, to innovate, to be fearless. This happens regardless of patents because it's an effect of good marketing and a clear understanding of the psychology of buyer behaviour.

I expected the Dragons to understand this since they, by the fire in their nostrils and the size of their bank balances, are victors in the mating game. In the Den, the combination of the availability bias and our genetic proximity to chimpanzees led to a temporary loss of judgement. Mercifully, Terrance and Trixie were nothing more than mute witnesses to the violence and suffered nothing more than a popped strap hook, which was easily repaired before they made their journey by private jet to Monaco.

I slept surprising well. I dreamt of knuckled Dragons running through dense forests, clamped fists pawing the ground as they ran. I woke when one of them turned and a familiar face lurched towards me, strap hook in hand.

In the morning, I spewed up what felt like gallons of mucus, took my medication and did my physiotherapy.

I felt good.

The Den felt a long way away. It felt manageable. I had a light break-fast, went back up to my room and called my PR agency. They said they could help. A disaster of any kind makes good news and my modest mauling was no exception.

I sat at the desk in my room and began scribbling on a branded hotel notepad:

Things I've Got Going for Me
I've still got a little bit of money left.
Trunkis are selling.
I've got growing interest in New York, Japan and Australia.
Meetings scheduled with Mothercare and many independent retailers.
The purchase order from the Museum of Modern Art arrived a few days ago.
I'm in control.
My lungs haven't packed up yet.

The list could have been longer but by the time I got to the bit about my lungs, I thought I'd got enough to be getting on with.

It took me less than week to sort out the strap hook. I asked the factory to mould it in a stronger plastic: so many wasteful battles fought that careful hands and clear minds can solve peacefully.

Three days after the ordeal in the Den, I noticed Jenny ordered another Trunki from my website. She was our biggest fan: she had at least three Trixies and five Terrances. It showed the power of the brand and the Trunki brand was about to be given the biggest test of its durability.

It began with a final trip to the warehouse to check all the catches had been replaced. They passed the test. After the inspection was over, I went home to watch the news. It was the 2006 World Cup in Germany. I'm not a keen football fan but World Cups don't leave much room for indifference unless your business collapses before the news anchor gets to the match report.

– Did you hear that? I said to my flat mate Paul who was eating the sweet and sour chicken I'd cooked.

– Yes, they're banning hand luggage. Good job nobody got hurt.

– Except me.

He looked at me like I was crazy, then his eyes opened:

– Oh, shit!

There it is again: the world changing faster than we can adapt. A plot had been uncovered to conceal liquid explosives in soft drinks and use them to blow up planes. The targeted flights were from London Heathrow to Canada and the United States. If they'd succeeded, 10,000 passengers might have been killed. As it was, the only thing destroyed was my business: all hand luggage was banned with immediate effect. 'The world's first and only ride-on suitcase for globetrotting tots' was now a major security threat.

I gave up on the news and went to my room to look online. It was worse than I imagined. Passengers travelling through any UK airport were allowed to carry a small list of items and they had to be in transparent plastic bags. I searched for a time limit on the ban. A week? A month? Then I read: 'the ban will be maintained indefinitely until circumstances change'. When Theo popped a strap hook, that was a problem I could solve. When the government banned hand luggage, that was completely out of my control. I don't know what vertigo feels like but it must be close to what I felt about one word bouncing around my head: indefinitely.

Within hours, the Trunki website was flooded with questions:

Is Trunki part of the luggage ban? Yes, we're afraid so.

My daughter's in tears – can she take Trixie on holiday with her? No, but Trixie loves to receive presents when she's left at home. It really cheers her up.

When will it end? We don't know.

I've just bought Terrance – can I get a refund? Unfortunately not, but the ban won't go on forever.

How do you know? Because forever is a very long time.

The following morning, I called the Department of Transport, the Home Office, the Department of Trade and Industry, EasyJet, Ryanair, British Airways, Virgin, searching for a tiny hole in 'indefinitely' where the horn of a Trunki might wedge its way through. When I got through to a government official, I played the best card I had:

– Do you know how upset this will make thousands of children. There'll be tears and . . .

– I'm sorry sir but . . .

– May I ask if you have any children?

He put the phone down.

I called my PR team. There was tutting and the occasional funereal blast of sympathy but they didn't know any more than me. I called my Dad to ask what he knew about it, and then apologised for wasting his time. My last resort was a list. It's what entrepreneurs do when they know they're screwed and they start thinking about how many buckets they need to get the water out of the lower deck before it reaches the helm and drowns the captain. The list started with *more exporting* and ended with *no payroll* and *no rent to pay*. The best bit was the sign off: 'I can keep the business going on a shoe string.' Shoe strings have been saviours and executioners of many businesses. It all depends how short they are. A fraction too long and it's a trip to the liquidator. I was sure mine were short enough. I breathed a sigh of relief. In a premonition of future disasters, not specifically related to me, I was taking back control.

I called David, my younger brother. He came down from Edinburgh where he was studying media studies. We batted ideas back and forth until we discovered the obvious: Trunki had been aimed at air travellers, now it was time to target domestic holiday-makers. Terrance and Trixie may no longer be allowed on planes but they had no problem getting access to campsites, caravan parks, piers, promenades and parks.

However, Margate, Llandudno and Center Parks were not enough as UK sales dropped dramatically but I started exporting to the USA, Japan, South Africa, Germany and Australia. I shipped 5,500 units internationally and it saved my cash flow. Then, with the suddenness with which the ban appeared, it was lifted. In September, the government announced that hand luggage was allowed back on board. God gives, God takes; I just wish he was more transparent in his decision-making.

That night I went for a run. The sky was clear and splashed with stars. My lungs were surprisingly free of mucus and, like a certified hysteric, I laughed uncontrollably.

I didn't laugh for long.

After filming Dragons' Den, the BBC said they'd give me six weeks' notice before the programme aired. We filmed in May and by the end of September the penultimate episode aired. As the episode came to a conclusion, hope with its twisted logic, gripped me. Perhaps they'd decided my humiliation wasn't worth showing. It was. At the end of the episode, there I was climbing the wooden staircase into the Dragons' lair. The following day I went to the newsagent's to get a copy of the *Radio Times*, turned to the day when Dragons' Den was on BBC2 and saw the headline, 'Wheelie Rubbish'. The colour drained from my face. This was bad. Worse than I could possibly have imagined.

For the second time in a matter of weeks, my business was on the verge of collapse. I made another list. *Things I Can Do*. Top of the list was telling my side of the story without sounding bitter. The spectre of unfairness haunts us all and there's nothing worse than the sugary, onanistic lamentations of jilted lovers and failed entrepreneurs. I felt my chest grinding. I coughed and, when it wouldn't stop, I went outside for air. I took deep breaths and when I came back I added to the list a short story, 'The Tale of Terrance, Trixie and the Five Dragons'. It didn't seem a formidable armoury to fight off the Dragons but it was all I had.

On the night the episode aired, my partner Kathryn, David and some close friends came to my flat to watch it. Over the last few months Kathryn and I had become very close. We met shortly after my relationship with Bec ended. 'Ended' is a chaste euphemism. The truth was, she dumped me. Despite the formulaic sadness, it gave me more time to develop Trunki and my business. That lasted until I met Kathryn. Before meeting her, I'd listen incredulously at lovesick friends talk about soulmates and kindred spirits and now I've got even less understanding of what they're talking about. It was Kathryn's dark-haired mysteriousness that drew me to her. To this day, she remains, in some part, unknowable to me, and that's the fuel that drives our relationship. Love isn't about looking at your partner and seeing through her like glass. What seduces and persists is a lover's elusiveness: the secrets we'll never know. Love is a deficit not a surplus of knowledge and that's what makes it wondrous.

As we sat in my flat, watching Dragons' Den, I hated every minute of it, especially where I said 'I didn't design that'. Pathetic. As the 'Wheelie Rubbish' descended into popped strap hooks and chimpanzee violence, I watched something remarkable happening on my laptop. I'd opened the stat counter on the Trunki website. It was getting more hits than it had ever got before. By the end of the night, the number of visitors was 350 times the maximum it had ever got in any night since the website launched. It got better. Every Trunki we had in stock sold. Our entire inventory sold out in one night.

Before the programme aired, I'd decided to put a survey on the Trunki website, asking kids and parents what they thought of the product. The response was overwhelming. Thousands of completed survey forms arrived in my inbox. Here's a sample:

> What we like most about Trunki is that it keeps the kids entertained at airports. We have two young girls and they never want to go anywhere without their Trunki.
> It's a very practical product, not only in the way it's fun for the children, but the way it's designed is really clever.
> Our children love the design, the colours. Thank you for creating a wonderful suitcase!
> I love Trixie. From Emma, aged 5.

I do public speaking all over the world and I still get choked up when I read these survey responses to an audience. It's not just what kids and their parents said about Trunki; it's *when* they said it. It happened minutes, hours and days after Dragons' Den aired. It could have been the breaking of my business. Instead, it was the making of it. I sold my entire inventory. I engaged a new generation of consumers. I mobilised those who already loved Trunki.

Over the weeks that followed, I tried to make sense of the positive response of consumers to the public rejection of Trunki by leading business experts. These were, of course, the days before trashing experts became a national sport and I don't question the success or treacherous journey all Dragons make to reach their destination. The fact remains, however, that they got it wrong. They took a piece of theatre by Theo Paphitis and lost their judgement. How?

There's a fascinating piece of research by the political scientist Philip Tetlock, who analysed more than 28,000 predictions made by 284 economic and political experts. The most startling outcome of the research was the discovery that overall forecast accuracy was what chance would expect to be the case and that the most inaccurate forecasts were made by experts with the highest media profiles. In other words, fame distorts judgement, which is why Dragons make mistakes.

Of course, what makes the Dragons successful is not the avoidance of error. It's the correction of error through relentless application and determination and, most of all, by being humble enough to change course. Years later, when Trunki became a global brand, Theo Paphitis came to Trunki Towers and said he didn't foresee such a successful outcome. Duncan Bannatyne also went on the record to say that 'the suitcase was the one we missed. Every time I'm in an airport I see them'.

The story of Trunki, like the story of anyone who battles against the odds, is the story of an underdog. Our culture is full of stories where the weaker defeats the stronger. In Malcolm Gladwell's book, *David and Goliath*, the defeat of the greater by the lesser is intended as a moral lesson in the power of *unreasonableness*. Gladwell quotes George Bernard Shaw: 'The reasonable man adapts himself to the world. The unreasonable man persists in trying to adapt the world to himself. Therefore all progress depends on the unreasonable man.' Taking the unreasonable path, the path laced with risk and uncertainty, is what entrepreneurs do. If they valued security over freedom, they'd work for a business rather than set one up themselves. By taking these risks, they live with the constant possibility of failure and destitution. I'm certain that being born with a terminal illness and watching my twin sister die gave me an advantage. I was born with a risk I didn't choose, whose consequences I was told, would be fatal. That inheritance rooted me in the present and drove my focus into relentless problem-solving. Like the wire-walker Philippe Petit, I know what it means to live life on a tightrope.

I've met people who suffer from terminal illnesses and I've watched many of them die. One of them was Jeff, who had cancer. Lying in his bed, not long before he died, he turned to me and said: 'Rob, people say I'm brave fighting this illness the way I have but that's not how I see it. What else could I do? Quit?' That, in a nutshell, is the psychology of how to overcome anything: treat it as a necessity and free yourself to fight in your own way.

In the month Dragons' Den aired on the BBC, I ran three half-marathons. I loved driving through the coughing and the pressure on my chest. The end was always a celebratory *Fuck you, CF!* when I crossed the finishing line and coughed up most of my lungs.

After the public responded so positively to my appearance I worked even harder and that took a heavy toll on my health. I took (most) of my medication (most) days and I (mostly) did my physiother-apy. I knew I had to rest but I refused to do so. I wouldn't concede defeat to CF nor did I want to miss the many business oppor-tunities that were opening up. I ended up wired to an IV line in my flat. I hated every minute of it. Like the lunchtimes at school when Kate and I were kept apart from the other kids and had to watch them playing outside while we had to manage our illness, being drip-fed drugs was a reminder of the fragility of my life. As usual, I worked on some designs and imagined new variations on the Trunki and then I decided I was well enough to detach myself from the line and get on with my life. Was I being brave or stupid? Neither. I was simply doing what was necessary.

I've no idea what the future will bring and I rarely, if ever, worry about it. I can't control it and I can't solve problems that belong in the future, so all I can do is focus on the present. As of today, I'm alive, my product is a global brand and my business is successful. Any or all of these things can change quickly and without notice, which is why it's so important to stay focused. In life, as in business, small details turn your world upside down. Most of those small details will arrive unforeseen, so all we can do is protect ourselves as best as we can against the risks we know about and be sufficiently flexible in our behaviour to adapt to those we don't. After all, our world is never as stable or as routinised as we think. Black Swans, as the mathematician and economist Nassim Nicholas Taleb called these sudden, unpredictable events, are likely to increase in frequency as global trading conditions became more volatile, along with our political and natural eco-systems.

I ended the year in manageable health with record sales and my business on a high. I'd survived a mauling in the Dragons' Den, Trunki had been banned, the Radio Times called it "Wheelie Rubbish' and my factory went bust. Still, I sure there was better to come, so it was with great anticipation that I spent the New Year planning my next move.

Self and Others

I can't breathe . . . I can't breathe . . . I can't breathe . . .

I repeat the words over and over in my head.

I wander down the corridor carrying Terrance under my arm, doing my best to look as normal as I can. A man passes me. He smiles. I think he's looking at me strangely but I'm probably imagining it. When he's gone and I'm sure no-one can see me, I press my hands against my chest. My heart's pounding. I feel sweat dripping through my shirt. A woman carrying a coffee smiles at me. I smile back, doing my best to look normal.

Except I'm crazy with pain.

I need a place to hide.

I try a meeting room door. It opens. I stagger in. I feel so weak and Terrance almost drops to the floor. Half a dozen suited heads turn towards a grown man with a toy under his arm and they are unsure whether to call for a priest, a doctor or security.

– Sorry . . . wrong room . . .

I must look like I've been on a month-long rave and taken a Trunki load of ecstasy.

There's a picture of stick man on a door at the end of the corridor. A toilet. I stagger through the door, find a cubicle, lock it behind me, close the lid and slump forwards.

I slither to the tiled floor and try to breathe. My whole body feels like it's being gripped by a fist.

– I'm not going to die in a toilet . . .

My words bounce around the cubicle, hurtling back to me like a dark boomerang.

The pain comes in waves like a raging sea, rising from my diaphragm, pounding my lungs and pressing on my chest like a concrete block.

I writhe on the ground, rolling from my left side onto my right.

I remember I'm here for a meeting. I've got a presentation prepared. I'm about to pitch Trunki to John Lewis. Terrance looks as content as he did when I carried him onto the train an hour ago.

– No chest pains for you, eh . . .

I lie still. The pain's easing. I manage to take a breath that goes down to the bottom of my rib cage before it's pushed up again. I want to vomit.

– Don't . . . please don't . . .

I don't know which part of my body I'm talking to but it ignores me. I throw up and as I stare into the toilet bowl the pain begins to ease. In a few minutes I'm on my feet, stumbling out of the cubicle. I catch my reflection in the mirror. I look like shit.

I take a handkerchief out of my pocket, wipe my brow, rearrange what little hair I've got left and gather myself.

I walk out.

A man smiles at me,

– Can I help you?

– Yes, I reply, surprised at my normality, I'm here to meet Will.

– He's in the office two doors on the right.

– Thank you.

I knock on the door and an hour later I come out again, smiling. I got the deal with John Lewis, my first major high street retailer. They agreed to run a pilot in 20 stores. When the purchase order came through a week later it was for hundreds of Trunkis. Someone had cocked up and my product was about to roll out across every John Lewis store in the UK.

As for the heartburn, it wasn't the first attack but it was the most severe and when I was rolling around on the toilet floor, it's one of the few times I've felt it was better to die than suffer senselessly. The feeling didn't last. As soon as I got to my feet, I wanted to live, like we all do when pain subsides. One of the biggest lessons I've learned by fighting a terminal illness is how necessary it is quickly to regain the will to fight for our lives after we've lost it, even for the tiniest fraction of time. Without that will to fight, we're finished.

The attack happened a few weeks after Dragons' Den aired and the ferocity with which I'd been driving myself, feeling I had to repay the faith children and their parents had shown in Trunki, proved more than my health could withstand.

After the attack of heartburn, I got back to my office in Bristol, otherwise known as my bedroom. I closed the curtains and lay in the dark. Everything was still. My breathing, slow and grinding, filled the air. I ran the events of the last few months over in my head and travelled, a second time, along the predictable path to my collapse. I'd eaten too much fat, had too many fry-ups, drunk too much coffee and run too many miles. For most people, having a fry-up is, at worst, a mild indulgence and drinking coffee is a necessary start to the working day. These simple pleasures are much more complex for someone with CF.

Why had I been so careless with myself? There's no doubt I live my life as if I'm normal. The drugs and the physio are an inconvenience, as is the fact that I should have died in my teens. I'm unlikely to live a long life but there are millions of people who feel perfectly well today who don't have a terminal illness, who'll die before they reach 50. I watched a clip of the writer Christopher Hitchens, shortly before he died of cancer in his early 60s. Speaking at an event, a member of the audience asked him how he was. 'Actually,' Hitchens replied, 'I'm dying.' Then, after a pause, he added, 'But then, so are you.'

My mind is always so alive and full of ideas that it's easy to resent my body for breaking down, for turning against me, for not working like it should. I hear my mother's voice reminding me how lucky I am. There are times when I want to silence that voice, scream back at it, tell it to shut up, but it stays with me, calm and relentless.

In the dark, I saw the shadows cast against the wall in my mind. I felt no emotion: just exhaustion. I fell asleep. When I woke up, I opened the curtains, it was dark outside. I put on my running kit. As I passed the mirror on my way out, I stopped and stared. Still breathing. Good.

Outside, the sound of my feet on the damp country roads felt reassuring. Every step grounded me. Occasional cars flashed by, lighting up the trees and hedgerows. When the inevitable coughing came and the pressure on my lungs grew, I ran through it. *Never give up, Rob, never give up.* Never giving up is easy to say. It's much harder to do.

A few weeks later, I moved the office out of my bedroom. I'd stayed from lack of money and the walls of my bedroom seemed to close further in on me by the day. I also needed to build a team, so I decided to hot desk in a friend's design studio in Bath.

The sales kept coming. The brand kept growing. Shortly after moving to Bath, I advertised for my first hire, a sales and marketing manager. This, too, was a humbling experience. I hired the man who was, without doubt, the best applicant for the simple reason that he was the only applicant, which proved that being told on television that your product is worthless has a more detrimental effect on recruitment than it does on sales.

James was young, a graduate, good-looking and laced with enthusiasm. He said he'd managed his own business in real estate. What that actually meant was he'd pushed his way into managing inventories for estate agents. Despite coming from a privileged background, he knew how to hustle and that's what I needed to drive the business forward.

I'd never employed anyone before and had no idea how to manage people, for two reasons: lack of experience and the fact that people came with messy, intractable problems that resisted solutions in ways that technical design problems did not. If I'd been wiser or less grateful for some support, I'd have known the relationship was finite from the start. However, all relationships, from a mismatched friendship to a doomed marriage, give the appearance of stability for the first few months at least.

In the three years that James worked for me, this is what happened:

– We went to Germany, America, Hong Kong and China, collecting hangovers and contacts.

– We cut deals with retailers and distributors and did a real-world MBA.

– He shagged a member of my team who left not long afterwards. I didn't like that.

– Then he asked for a substantial stake in the business and that was The End.

That was my first and biggest lesson in holding boundaries in business. James worked hard, he was funny and charismatic as well being a reasonably effective salesman. Above all, he was my friend.

My first mistake lay in not understanding the power of one tiny word to create confusion: the word 'we'. When he said 'we', he saw no difference between us in our relation to Trunki and the business I'd created and funded. When I said 'we', I saw a working relationship with a friend who was also an employee. The confusion wasn't helped by the fact that he was my first employee, so I shouldn't have been surprised two and a half years later when he asked for a big slice of my business. Except I was surprised. My lack of emotional intelligence meant I struggled to understand where he was coming from. How could he expect shares in the business just because he'd closed some deals and worked hard? That's what I paid him to do. He hadn't invested or raised any money. He got paid every month even when I withheld my own wages to pay the rest of the team, which numbered eight by the time he left.

He burst into my office.

– Fuck you, Rob. How can you not see what I've done for you?

– I appreciate what you've done for me but I can't give you free shares in the company?

– Can't?

– Won't.

– Fuck you.

I can't blame this collapse in our relationship on his background or his character. It was my fault. I'd assumed he understood he worked for me. I never asked him to defer his wages nor did I ever sell him short on his bonuses. He worked, I paid him well and that was the basis of our relationship. Except we were great mates and that's where my naivety created confusion. I missed the gulf between my understanding of our respective relationships to the business and his. The consequences were as unpleasant as they were inevitable. In his resignation email he wrote: '. . . I can't believe you've treated me this way after all we've been through together. You wouldn't be where you are without me and I hope you never forget that . . .'

I wanted to write back telling him that I'd never promised him any-thing other than a good salary and job security, a promise I'd hon-oured even when cash was short. I never asked him for any money nor did I expect him to take the pressure that was mine to take as the owner of the business.

When you run a growing business, there's always pressure on cash and I saw my job as managing director to protect James and my other employees from those pressures. Even when I felt anxious about the future, I kept those feelings to myself. Despite this, we're all wrapped up in our own version of the world and have a sense of our own worth, which may or may not be grounded in reality. Because we're closer to our own emotional struggles and challenges than we are to the struggles of other people, it distorts our thinking.

After James left, I never made that mistake again. The difference between an entrepreneur and an employee has nothing to do with hard work or ability. It has to do with an attitude to risk which can be summarised easily: if you are prepared to risk everything you own on a gamble that you can run a successful business, if you can cope with the pressure of having the responsibility to look after those who work diligently for your brand, if you can wing-it in the face of seemingly insurmountable odds, then start a business. If you can't, then work for one. It's your choice but, whichever choice you make, accept the rules you've got to play by and live your life as best as you can.

Despite the problems with my health, by the end of 2007, a year after my humiliation in the Den, I'd got myself into the ridiculous state of feeling invincible. I'd built a small but growing worldwide distributor network and consumers loved Trunki. I paid people well, I loved my team but I never considered selling any shares. For any business person, they're the last thing you let go and you do so only if you feel a cash crisis is insurmountable or if you're made an offer you can't refuse.

Every day, kids and their parents flooded the Trunki website with tales of their positive experiences. By now the Trunki family numbered four: Terrance, Trixie, Frieda the Cow and Tipu the Tiger, who we took on a day trip to Longleat to meet Soundari, a real three-year-old Siberian tiger. After packing Tipu with meat, we placed him in Soundari's enclosure and watched as the Siberian tiger picked Tipu up in her teeth and carried him by the handles into the long grass. By this time, we were worried for Tipu's safety but Soundari licked him as if he was one of her own cubs. The mothering was so intense that Soundari's rough tongue erased Tipu's stripes. The video of that encounter is one of the most popular we've posted on YouTube and has been watched more than 350,000 times.

This was everything a brand should be and, because of this success, I'd locked myself inside my head with delusions of invincibility, which are always a prelude to personal and professional disaster. 'If you are not humble,' the boxer Mike Tyson said, 'then humbleness will visit itself upon you,' and I was overdue a visit.

The visit came when I tried to break into the United States. Despite the Special Relationship™ and the smiles, I knew the knives that sliced the apple pie were sharp enough to cut my business into pieces. So, without capital or allies on the ground, I decided to license Trunki to a large North American toy company based in Canada. It seemed an easy move to make. I flew to Toronto. The meeting went well. In business, on the odd occasion when people make rational decisions, those decisions are driven by mutual self-interest and this was an opportunity for us all to make money. They identified the need to redesign some aspects of Trunki to meet US toy standards and I came back to them with Trunki MK3. Up until this point, Trunki had failed part of the USA toy safety standard called the Topple Test. The seat was too long and could cause children to fall off. By shortening the seat, I solved two problems: children could ride Trunki safely and, by cutting grooves at both ends of the shortened seat, Trunki would no longer need to be displayed on the ground or on the top shelf, which meant it was missed by many customers. It could now be stacked in stunning displays made of towers and pyramids without the need for any additional point of sale material.

They were impressed. We shook hands and they agreed to send me a contract before I took the flight home.

When the contract arrived, it wasn't as agreed, so I called them:

– It's not what we agreed.

– We reviewed the meeting and if you want to get into the US, you need to put Trunki in Walmart.

– I won't do it for launch. It cheapens the brand.

– The brand isn't named right for the US market. Trunki won't work over here and we want the right to change the name.

– That's not going to happen.

– Who do you think you are? Apple?

– No.

– Then we might as well call it a day.

– OK, let's do that.

So that's what we did.

I felt they'd devalued the brand and failed to understand the power of Trunki. They felt I'd overplayed my hand and lost touch with commercial reality. In the end, perhaps we were both right but the consequence was that Trunki didn't get into the US at the first attempt.

Whenever I make a decision, right, wrong or completely crazy, I've always been able to accept the consequences. I don't blame other people for my failures but I do acknowledge their contribution to my success. However, on the flight back from Toronto, I kept thinking about how the meeting ended.

Who do you think you are?

It wasn't a question I ever asked myself and it felt uncomfortable. I know how to answer practical questions and solve practical problems like how to build a brand. I know if you want a retail brand to be consumed by ABC1s, then think carefully about Eisner's 'thousand small gestures': is it in the right outlet? Is it packaged distinctively? Does it have a powerful story to tell?

Asking – Who do you think you are? – is a different kind of question. It felt like a low blow.

I often feel I'm a mystery to myself, as if I don't really know who I am. If you were to ask me I'd say I'm a good problem solver, I think I'm kind and good humoured. Beyond that, the question doesn't make much sense to me.

So, as the flight crossed the Atlantic carrying a dent in my cloak of invincibility, the US market felt more remote than ever. It was an overnight flight and, despite my tiredness, I couldn't sleep. I looked out of the window. The sky was dark and clear. In the distance, I saw the flashing light of another plane and felt a wave of loneliness wash over me. I saw the path my life had taken, twisting this way and that and, whenever I saw it, I was walking alone. Despite the love and support of my parents, the connection to Kate that will always survive her death and the many people who have helped, supported and worked with me, the path of an entrepreneur is, by definition, a solitary one. Driven by two conflicting emotions, a need for control and a capacity for risk, entrepreneurs push forward relentlessly, often accumulating risks that they bury in the belief they have the resilience to manage them. Sometimes it works; mostly it doesn't, but we drive on regardless.

For me, the ultimate solitariness of running my own business also drove me to solitary sports like cycling, swimming and running because they connect me to the world and disconnect me from it at the same time. I've also realised this feeling of being an 'outsider' is not far from the criminal mind. Ever since I first watched the film, *The Loneliness of the Long-Distance Runner*, the opening scene has stayed with me. Shot in black and white, the scene features the protagonist, Colin Smith, running against a cloudy sky. Over the relentless sound of his steps beating against the road, we hear his voice:

> Running's always been a big thing in our family, especially running away from the police. It's hard to understand. All I know is you've got to run, running without knowing why through fields and woods. And a winning post's no end, even though barmy crowds might be cheering themselves daft. That's what the loneliness of the long-distance runner feels like.

The film follows Colin, who comes from a troubled home. When he gets incarcerated in a detention centre for juvenile offenders, he's encouraged to run by the governor, who sees the talent the boy possesses. Supported by the governor, Colin becomes the star runner and, in the film's finale, he's chosen to represent the detention centre in a race against privileged boys from a public school. Leading the race, Colin stops before crossing the finishing line, allowing the upper class boys to win. Enraged by what he sees as an act of betrayal, the governor puts Colin back to work in the machine shop, his favouritism at an end along with any aspirations he had to run.

It's easy to see the film as a morality tale, rich against poor, favourite against underdog, but what stayed with me was Colin's defiance. He ran to escape, from his past, from himself, and that impulse followed him through his life. He valued his freedom over any security or status the governor could provide and he wasn't prepared to sacrifice that freedom at any cost. That is what drives me. I can't imagine a life where I can't explore my creativity, regardless of the personal or financial cost. What point is there in living without trying to live at least one dream, however unrealistic and fraught with risk that dream might be?

The biggest risk by far of running a business is running out of cash. Most start-ups fail not because the products are bad or the service is poor (although plenty of businesses do fail for these reasons). They fail because the owners underestimate the cash required to get the business off the ground. They set a budget, skewed by optimism, and expect everything to happen as planned. When it doesn't, they're left having to raise more cash and it's always more difficult to raise cash a second time when the only reason you need it is because you miscalculated how much cash your business needed the first time.

In my case, these calculations were straightforward. For the first six months, I'd survived by borrowing £40,000. After proving the business model, I borrowed a further £150,000 in two tranches from the bank without having to give a personal guarantee. In any event, my only asset was a mountain bike. I spent the cash on two things: buying inventory (the bank also gave me letters of credit, which meant I got longer payment terms from the manufacturer) and travelling to the USA, China and the EU to set up deals with distributors. The time I spent travelling meant my physio suffered. I can't just sit back on planes vibrate my lungs and cough up mucus. Again, the result of my neglect was a decline in my health, which served to remind me to take my drugs and do my physio. Then, my health picked up and the cycle of neglect began all over again and always, in the background, was the same dilemma: how far to go it alone, when to ask for help.

I didn't always go it alone because I thought I knew best. Sometimes I went it alone because I couldn't stand any intrusion behind the wall in my mind. So I never told my staff I had CF. I coughed. They saw me struggle for breath. But I refused to tell them I had CF because

977 Mum with her 6-month-
old twins. We arrive a month
early on her 30th birthday and
were diagnosed with CF at
2 weeks. After 4 months we
escaped hospital and were
allowed to go home.

1980 In my 'Element' while
helping Dad restore a Welsh
chapel.

1981 Smiling on our first day at school, unaware of how difficult schooling would turn out to be.

1994 Kate and I in Canada after her successful transplant. She died four months later.

1995 Test riding my A-level design project, the Prodigy recumbent bike. I came top in a class of one.

1996 The Bug furniture range dad commissioned for his office, sculpted in plywood and inspired by insect legs.

1997 Receiving the first Trunki award (then called Rodeo) from the chairman of the Institute of Materials at the BASF Plastic Design Awards.

Concept
Ride-On Suitcase

DESIGNED FOR 2-6 YEAR OLD'S

SECRET COMPARTMENT CONSEALED BY DOOR MOLDED TO MAIN BODY BY LIVE HINGE.

SIDE

STEEL PIN PIVITS HINGE

STABILIZER

SECRET COMPARTMENT ALSO PREVENTS TIPPING BACKWARDS

SCOOP FOR HANDLE

RIDGE ADDS STRENGTH

SADDLE

FOAM LIP PREVENTS DAMAGE TO FINGERS

OPEN

FLAT FOLDING HANDLE

FOAM EXTRUSION

HORN HANDLE

3D FRONT

CLIP CAR DOOR STYLE

WHEELS SNAP FIT OVER PLASTIC AXLE.

Rodeo

2002 Trunki concept sketches made after being released from hospital in Australia.

2006 On 5th May, the first container of 1,400 Terrance and Trixies arrives at Avonmouth docks. This date is now celebrated as Trunki's official birthday.

2006 With my brother Dave at our first tradeshow at the NEC.

2006 In the Den shortly after Theo broke the strap hook: am I facing the fire of five Dragons or the mania of a troop of chimpanzees?

2009 Three years after he broke the strap hook, Theo visits Trunki Towers for a BBC follow-up show called *Where Are They Now?* I gave him a Hercules Trunki with padlocks replacing the hooks.

2008 Real tiger love: Tipu being carried by Saundari at Longleat Safari Park before having his stripes licked off!

2012 Promotion photoshoot inspired by the film *Chariots of Fire* for the launch of Jack, our official London 2012 Trunki.

2011 A major landmark: a space-themed party at The Mothership to celebrate 1 million Trunki sold.

A Royal Appointment for a Trunki in disguise, as he makes friends with one of the Queen's corgis.

2011 Meeting the Queen who presented me with an MBE and asked about the little suitcases made for children.

Family photo at Windsor Castle with mum, Kathryn and dad.

2013 Celebrating the BGF
investment and becoming,
against all odds, a millionaire
by doing what I love.

2015 The Trunki team outside
The Mothership after our graffiti
summer party. A local street
artist painted the side of the
building and we did some
colouring and tagging.

2012 Presenting Sir Richard Branson with his very own Virgin Galactic Trunki at his garden party, celebrating being named as one of the 100 fastest growing companies in the UK.

2013 Celebrating my first and last court victory in the Great Trunki War against PMS. In case you're confused, the product on the right is the Trunki, the one on the left is the copy. It's obvious they haven't stolen my design – right?

2014 My number one fan supporting me running a triathlon.

2016 At last: running a profitable UK factory, making a production run of Bluebell the Pony Trunki.

2015 Ida playing at the Trunki Museum at my grandparents house, where every design ever made is kept.

2020 The Trunki Dungeon where copies are kept under lock and key at The Mothership. Despite their crimes, we treat them well and torture is forbidden!

2018 Rafe spots himself on the front page of the *Sunday Times* business supplement after we announced strong financial results.

2019 Ida and Rafe riding the new Trunki folding bike and scooter, which they inspired me to create.

2018 Sharing my story of defying the odds at the UWE Distinguished Address Series to local businesses and students.

2020 Rafe, Kip and Ida: the children I was told I'd never have.

1. Ida and Rafe on their new Trunki wheels. 2. PR shot at Bristol Airport for the Times. 3. Me, Ida & Rafe on our way to board a flight. 4. Me on the panel at a debate on startups at the British Library. 5. Honorary Doctorate at Bath University. 6. Winning SME of the Year at the National Business Awards. 7. Launching Paddington Trunki at a Chinese trade show. 8. The Trunki rainbow wall showcasing the travel gear range. 9. Tipu the Tiger ready to pounce outside the Supreme Court. 10. Benny the Cat meets his imposter Trunki. 11. Gruffalos being made in Plymouth. 12. My first office in Bath.

I hated the thought of them having sympathy for me. Then one day James walked in and said,

– You know they know don't you?

– Know what?

– That you're dying.

– What?

– Only joking . . . that you've got CF.

– I don't want them to know.

– Rob, you'd better get real on this one. You can't hide it when your lungs are coming out of your mouth.

– You mean they noticed?

– Just a bit!

– What did they say?

– What you'd expect . . . Is he alright? What's the matter with him?

– So you took it upon yourself to tell them.

– Like any friend would do.

I paused.

– Thanks James.

– Anytime.

I felt better when I knew they knew. It got a monkey off my back and we could get on with building a business and I was determined to make the business culture as much fun as the product. Stealing an idea from Innocent drinks, I created unusual job titles like sales superstar, sales sheriff, graphics genius, admin extraordinaire, Miss Moneypenny, marketing whizz and the chairperson became known as the intergalactic ambassador.

International sales kept growing and more recruits came into the business. I hired Kathryn to manage customer service and HR. Despite her ability, this was a decision fraught with risk. The blurred boundaries between our personal and professional lives caused problems but I didn't know the rules to play by: I was making it up as I went along.

As the business grew, I felt a strong need to connect with other business people. Self was not enough. I needed others. At a local Prince's Trust event I was introduced to a group of business and community leaders that met as part of an organisation called Footdown. There were about 15 of us in the group, an eclectic mix of entrepreneurs, company directors, charity directors, police officers, all united by a desire to learn more about how to lead organisations well. They initially gave me access for free. I thought it was because they liked me. The truth was that Stuart, a shipping entrepreneur from the group, had paid for the sessions. The physicist Isaac Newton famously claimed that he saw further than others because he stood on the shoulders of giants. Stuart taught me a different lesson, that much of our success is down to the help we receive from people whose kindness is unrecorded in history books.

The Footdown meetings were useful because they were structured and formulaic. Each meeting followed the same pattern. A guest speaker ran the morning session and, in the afternoon, members shared their challenges and got feedback from the group. In my second session, I stood up in front of the group, all of them older than me, many of them successful and respected leaders in business and public life.

I coughed.

– I'm here . . . I said (cough) . . . because I'm tired of winging it and I want to know how to run a business properly.

To my surprise everyone laughed.

I didn't know what to say, then Stuart said,

– That *is* running a business properly. We're all winging it! How else do you run a successful business?

Because of their candour and cynicism I learned so much from that group. They may have been winging it but they passed on nuggets of information that I absorbed like a sponge and applied at Trunki. I bought books for my staff. I can't remember them all, but *Who Moved My Cheese?* was one and *Eat That Frog* was another. Perhaps the most important was *Good to Great*. I wanted every member of the Trunki team to grow and develop with the business. I reasoned that the happier they were, the more attention I gave them, the more they'd care and the longer they'd stay.

Investment in people also helped me learn quickly those who were good for the business and those who weren't. I grew a tougher skin and didn't hesitate to decline a candidate, regardless of the strength of their CV, if they didn't buy into the culture or if they weren't up for the Trunki journey. Before inviting prospective candidates to an interview, I'd ask what they were passionate about. If I felt they lacked passion, I wouldn't ask them in. You can gain experience but you can't learn passion and apathy kills businesses. You can't hang on to people who drain the energy out of your business. If you hire a bad apple and keep them in the hope that the other members of the team will help them improve, you're going to be disappointed when the opposite inevitably happens: one weak, disruptive member of any business team will be more likely to pull the rest of the team down to his or her level than be raised up by them. Firing people may be brutal but when you're responsible for an entire team, if you don't act to remove disruptive people, your best people will leave and you'll be left as the captain of a sinking ship run by an incompetent crew who don't care if it sinks.

I'm always humble enough to change direction and the team was fearless in telling me if I was being an idiot. That's another reason you need other people: if you listen only to yourself, you'll never learn anything except how to repeat the same mistakes. If you want to sustain yourself and your business, your first priority is to invest, emotionally and financially, in the people that work for you because they're the people who'll keep your customers happy. It's like a gene pool in biology: the bigger it is, the stronger the individual organism will be.

One thing I hated and never understood was office gossip. Why would somebody open their mouth to spew negativity about someone else? Why can't people just get on? This was another example of how my practical, problem-solving mind struggles with any behaviour that doesn't end with a viable solution.

In 2007, we moved into Trunki Towers, our first office. But, despite this growth, there were still financial problems to overcome. There were months when I struggled to meet the payroll (although if anyone ever went short, it was me and only me) and, in 2009, I decided to sell 10% of the business to a successful businessman for £200,000, twice what I'd asked for on Dragons' Den. We could now move to larger premises, which we called The Mothership. It was more of playground than an office with slides and break-out areas accessed by climbing up spiral staircases. Hundreds of Trunki pictures, starring smiling children, covered the walls along with fake windows looking out to space. The business was set for massive expansion. Trunki was going to take over the world.

After I received the investment, Theo Paphitis, came to see how I was getting on. Alone, he was personable and kind. When he arrived I presented him with a bespoke Trunki called Hercules with padlocks instead of strap hooks. The BBC filmed his visit and after he left I put the footage on YouTube. The video ends with my first investor handing over £200,000 for 10% of the business, valuing Trunki at £2 million just three years after the Dragons deemed it worthless.

The investment also allowed me to take BoostApak to market. After listening to parents moaning about the hassle of taking their child's car seat on holiday or, even worse, having to hire a used sick-stained seat, I sensed an opportunity to solve their problem, I invented a children's car seat with storage space for travel essentials that doubled up as a backpack. I partnered with a design consultancy that specialised in car seat engineering and the result was a hugely successful product that's won many awards, including a Mumsnet Best Award, a Practical Parenting & Innovation Award and Best Travel Invention Award.

Yet, despite my success, there was something missing. I fought my battles by relying on my own resources and, increasingly, by recognis-ing my need for support from other people. Principal among these was Anne, a retired police officer who, as part of my Footdown mem-bership, became my coach. After I'd sold 10% of the business she asked me how I felt.

– It gives the business financial stability, I can . . .

– That's not what I'm asking. I asked how you felt.

– I can launch new products like BoostApak.

– You're not listening, Rob: how do you feel?

– The wages are . . .

– How do you *feel*?

I started coughing and her questions gave me a migraine. I cut the meeting short. It's not that I didn't have any language for emotion. I just couldn't afford to use it. I had to keep my wall intact.

A few months later, at a two-day Footdown retreat run by a speaker called Nigel Risner, we had to identify a difficult conversation we'd been putting off. We split into pairs and sat facing each other, knee to knee. There was nowhere to hide. Mike, a successful entrepreneur, asked me what was holding me back in my life.

– Guilt, I said, completely unaware of where that word came from.

– About what?

– About leaving Great Ormond Street Hospital after my sister Kate died. I let my parents down and I abandoned Kate.

– Are your parents still alive?

– Yes they are.

– Have you spoken to them about how you feel?

– I can't . . .

– Can't?

– I don't know how . . .

– Is that the difficult conversation you've been putting off?

The wall collapsed and I burst into tears.

Guilt and Forgiveness

The sky, overcast and grey, presses on the three of us, me, my mother and father, as we walk through the cemetery gate. I don't think we speak. If we do, it's only to defer the purpose of our visit.

I've brought us here to settle accounts. It's what the grief-stricken do. At some point in our lives, if we are lucky, we draw up a ledger of our life. On one column are the credits. These may be virtues like honesty, decency and generosity, which we list along with instances of how we apply them in our lives. On the second column are the debits. Generally, this is a shorter list. It can afford to be because the weight of the debit column is always greater. One debit for every ten credits. The transition from credit to debit is done in two words: *Yes but . . .* This is how it works:

> I made a promise to my mother. Yes, but . . .
> I treat people well. Yes, but . . .
> I keep the promises I make. Yes, but . . .

It's what comes after the 'yes but' that overwhelms the credit column. In my case, it was one action: 'Yes but, I left Kate in Great Ormond Street and went back to Loughborough University.' It can take a lifetime to draw up this ledger, which is why most of us never settle accounts with ourselves. It's the hardest deal to cut and many fall long before the final balance is agreed. I can think of reasons why I'm doing it now. I can point to Anne forcing me to face my feelings, to my mentors at Footdown making me face what's holding me back, but the real reason is I have to do it. If I don't do this, I know I'll get sick. 'Yes but, you'll get over it, just move on with your life . . .' If I could take that advice I would but I can't. Guilt is the debit that won't let me rest or face the future and I've brought my parents here to tell them.

We get closer to Kate's grave. I haven't been here for a long time. I don't like being here now. It's cold and I don't know how to begin. I think it's twenty years, perhaps more, since I spoke, meaningfully, to my parents about Kate.

I swallow hard. Mum puts her arm in mine.

– I . . .

– It's okay darling, she says.

– I . . . don't know how to do this . . . or what to say . . . I feel so guilty about leaving you and Kate . . . I didn't know what to do and I didn't want to be there . . . I wanted her to live and she was dead so I went back to Loughborough and left her and I couldn't bear it . . .

I know I'm speaking too fast. I start crying.

– You did the right thing darling, absolutely the right thing.

Dad puts his hand on my back.

– We're so proud of you, Rob.

– I need to move on for me too. I want a future and this has been holding me back, without me even knowing it . . .

I bury feelings because they're dangerous for me. Only now, do I feel they're far more dangerous *because* they're buried. I know this won't be the first of a miserable trail of *mea culpas*. I'm doing this to be able to not have to do it again, a homage I won't allow to become a perpetual wake.

The mood lightens and we talk about what Kate might be doing if she was alive. Reading, for sure, and working with children. She loved kids, their spontaneity. Perhaps she saw in them a future she was denied or a capacity for play that took weight out of the world.

I don't know how long we stay in the cemetery. It's easier to leave that it was to arrive. The ledger feels more balanced and there's no sense in letting myself be pulled back into a hospital room in Great Ormond Street for the rest of my life. 'So we beat on,' Scott Fitzgerald writes at the end of *The Great Gatsby*, 'boats against the current, born ceaselessly into the past.' Who does this indulgence serve? I don't think about my future in terms of its length. Others, no doubt, will do that for me and the line will probably be shorter than most. For me, the challenge is not to live long. I have no control over that. The challenge is to live well, which means refusing to be pulled back into the past.

Settling accounts isn't an endless process of wrapping myself in sackcloth and ashes and wailing, helplessly, until I get bored of my own grief. It's about knowing our ledgers are weighted towards the debit column, regardless of its length, and moving on means restoring as much balance as we can.

'Yes, but you abandoned Kate . . .'

I didn't abandon her. Leaving the hospital, driving back to Loughborough, going to the pub with my classmates, wasn't about her. It was about me. I want to live and that was the best way I knew how. In the end, settling accounts with ourselves is an act of kindness and, when we add up the two columns, we can't afford to indulge the negative. For me, perhaps for all of us, living well means remaking the past. Taking my parents to the cemetery, telling them what I'd been carrying for over twenty years, was a means to honour, not forget, Kate. Perhaps, at some point, I'll feel the need to do this again but I doubt it. If I do, I'll be abandoning myself and that will be hard to forgive. The voice pleading 'Yes but' will always be with me, as it is with all of us. All I can do is make it softer, less insistent. I'll do this by letting it know I understand what it's asking of me and in response I'll say, 'I'm not my guilt. I never was and I never will be. Now let's move on . . .'

Pregnancy and Productivity

Move on.

But where to?

I spoke to Anne.

– What do you want, Rob? What are you doing all this for?

As soon as she asked it, I wish she hadn't. The question was too big for me.

– I want security.

– Security?

– Financial security.

The answer was reasonable, partially true and I said it with conviction. I hoped she'd accept my answer and move on.

No chance.

Anne hadn't risen to the top of the police force without knowing how to interrogate a prisoner.

– Is that it? she asked.

– No.

– What else do you want, Rob?

– I think I want a family, kids.

– Think?

– I *know* I want a family and kids.

I felt numb.

Years earlier, when I was 19, I'd found out by accident that I couldn't have children. Skint and at university, my mates and I decided we'd earn extra money by donating sperm to a sperm bank. When we arrived at the hospital, we stumbled in one at a time. When it came to my turn, the nurse asked a few details. It all went well until she asked,

– Do you suffer from any illness or take any medication?

– Yes, I have cystic fibrosis.

She stopped tapping her keyboard and looked up at me.

– Is that a problem? I asked.

– I'm afraid it is. We can't take your sperm, Rob, and not just because of the risk of passing on the illness. Men with cystic fibrosis struggle to conceive children.

Later, my mother confirmed what the nurse had told me.

– It's the mucus in your body, she said. It stops your pancreas working and blocks your tubes.

– Then why can't they unblock them? I asked.

– It's not that easy, darling.

Until now, confronted with the purpose of my life by Anne, I had not thought about having children. My practical mind accepted the fact that I couldn't have kids so there was no point in thinking about it or waiting for the medical profession to make it possible. Mum always used to tell us they'd find a cure for CF but, after many false dawns, I gave up on that idea too. My life was as it was and I had no choice other than to accept it.

But now something gnawed at me.

– It doesn't surprise me, Anne said. You're such a big kid yourself, you've made a product for kids and you're great with kids. Of course you want kids.

Her directness and the fact that she'd seen in me what I couldn't admit to myself, shocked me.

– But I can't have children, I said apologetically.

– Can't?

I didn't answer. I don't believe in God or an afterlife but I do believe children give us a kind of immortality. They are our self and our other, me and not-me. By bringing them into the world, we create the only hope we have of a better, sustainable future and I confessed to myself that I wanted children more than I wanted anything.

By 2010, we were selling more than 250,000 Trunkis a year in every corner of the globe.

I was running half-marathons and competing in triathlons.

I was in love with Kathryn.

If ever there was a time to have children, it was now.

All my life, I'd lived beyond the limits of my illness. I refused to see it as a limitation and, when I came across things I couldn't do, like become an astronaut, I accepted it and moved on. My practical mind saw no point in wasting energy on what I couldn't control. Everything else I challenged.

Now, for the first time in my life, I wanted to change something that wasn't in my power to change. A hunger for something over which I had no power gripped me and refused to let go.

In November 2010, Kathryn and I took a holiday in Cuba. It was the first holiday I'd taken in four and a half years. Cuba was unlike any-where I'd ever been. Music floating down narrow, crumbling streets, bars unchanged for generations, a culture untouched by Coca-Cola and McDonald's.

– There's no point in talking about it, Kathryn.

– I know there isn't, but . . .

– There's no point in talking about what isn't going to happen.

Then the first message came.

> Her Majesty's Government would like to speak to you. Please can you contact Mr. Perry.

I tried to reply. There wasn't a signal. Up until that moment, the erratic Wi-Fi and phone signal in Cuba had been a blessing. Now I stared at my phone, not knowing what to do.

I ran through a list in my head of what the government might want me for. It was a short list:

Tax.

I knew I'd paid more than my share of tax. I didn't have any offshore accounts. I had no hidden assets. If there was a problem it had to be Bill, the company accountant. He was pleasant. Too pleasant perhaps. He was fair but was he hiding something? A nice guy, but was it a mask? Aren't all good fraudsters charming? The more I let my imagination lose its anchor with reality, Bill changed from a competent bean counter to a satanic number cruncher.

– What do you think of Bill? I asked Kathryn.

– He's lovely.

– Mmmm.

– What are you mmmm-ing about?

I told her.

She laughed.

I laughed with her.

– Mr Law, the concierge said as we walked into the lobby of our hotel, There's a message for you . . .

– From the government?

– Yes, how did you know that?

It was the same message I'd received by text.

At just after three, I got a strong signal on my phone. I dialled voice-mail. The message began the same as the text then it cut off. The man spoke with a voice that belongs in a government department, confident, sure of its place in the world, brimming with pomp, circum-stance and perfect diction. He asked me to call him back. It was too late. I'd call in the morning.

We had dinner on a balcony overlooking Havana. A strong wind blew and the sounds of the city rose and fell like thunder.

– All I know, I said to Kathryn, is it's nothing to do with Bill.

In the morning, there was another message. This time it didn't break. I listened to it twice.

> It's Michael Perry here again and I'd like you to be so kind as to call me back and let me know if you would be willing to accept an Honour from Her Majesty. You have been nomi-nated to became a Member of the British Empire for services to business and Her Majesty would be delighted if you chose to accept.

There are two ways of receiving a message like that. The first is the way you are expected to receive it, with pride, elation and a pretence of humility. The second is the way I received it: delight at the thought of Mum and Dad having a day out at Buckingham Palace. In the same way as I spent my life feeling the pain of others before my own, I did the same with joy. Things might be good or they might be bad, but whichever way the dice rolled my feelings were rarely about myself. This isn't because I'm making a bid for sainthood in recognition of a selfless life. It's the emotional opposite. I feel for others because I *can't* feel for myself. Show me a child suffering on television and I'll weep or turn away. Tell me I'm going to die of CF and I'll challenge you, I'll tell you I'll fight until my last breath, but the last thing I'll do is cry. And there's no emotional heroism in that. It's just a matter of survival.

Kathryn was proud of me.

Dad didn't know what to say.

– That's wonderful, Mum said before adding, What have you done to deserve that?

One of the many lessons I learned from Mum was to keep myself grounded at all times and to believe the world was a meritocracy. Even her son had to earn his rewards. However, it would have hurt her to know that I felt I didn't deserve it. I thought about the people who'd shared their lives with me. Some, like my sister Kate, I loved to the point of silence. Others, like the business group at Footdown, I respected as peers and mentors. What they all had was a greater right to recognition than me. At the time of writing this book, Trunki, the product and the business, has received more than 140 awards. I take great delight in those awards because they're for all of us. They let me bury my inability to delight in my own success by enjoying the success of the team that made it possible. The MBE was different. It was for me and all I wanted to do was give it to someone else.

I told three people, Kathryn, Mum and Dad. I made it clear they had to remain silent until the honours were announced in the January 2011 New Year's Honours List. They did as they were told. I like to think it was my threat to put them in the Tower that forced their silence. In reality, it was what Mum called, 'respect'. That's a word that once belonged to a forgotten age before it was revived by 'the street'. For me, the absence of respect leads to fracture and division. While I write this, the country, Parliament and the business community, are tearing each other apart over Brexit. But Brexit never was the real issue. It was a scream, a rallying call, for those who felt they'd been denied respect, whose lives passed unnoticed under the inevitable drift towards globalisation. When you strip people of respect and the dignity that goes with it, they'll strip you of the right to live undisturbed by their protests. In business, if you hire someone and keep them on because they're good for your business, you must give them the respect they've earned, or they'll get resentful and resentment kills all relationships, personal and professional, more surely than any other emotion.

So, January began with the announcement. Mum, having told the world 100 times over in her head, now went about doing it for real like the ultimate Town Crier. Then she said:

– That's enough of that. Now you're an MBE, don't forget you're just like everyone else.

With Mum, it always came down to that. How could I forget I was just like everyone else? Fit, healthy, well and blessed. *Fuck you, CF*.

If the year began well, I decided to make it more difficult.

First, I went with Kathryn to see a doctor about IVF, then, about a year later, I bought a factory. Other than that, they were both about improving productivity and fraught with danger; there was little to link the two decisions but the fate of one seemed to track the other between the announcement of the MBE in January 2011 and the end of 2013.

The journey to the IVF clinic began years earlier, when Kathryn and I had been dating for about a month. In much the same way as

I believed I was hiding my illness from my staff, despite the fact that I coughed most of my guts up onto my office desk, I thought I'd managed to hide it from Kathryn, for at least the first few weeks of our relationship. This is where I, and I suspect men more generally, can be remarkably stupid.

So, I decided it was time to tell her about CF. This was a delicate subject so I planned the revelation down to the last detail. Where? A restaurant. Clean linen, a chocolate-glazed, plateful of dopamine. Perfect. How? It may be ancient history and unknown to a generation of teenage tech wizards but I buy into Marshall McLuhan's famous theory about the medium being more important than the message. My first choice of medium was text. I decided I'd send it just before she arrived at the restaurant so she'd read it before we sat down for dinner. I tried half a dozen variations of which the best was: *I've got 65 Roses XOXO R x*. Mercifully, something stopped me from sending it. Finally, I settled for a more primitive medium: my voice.

I made my declaration of illness as if it was just another problem to solve.

– There's something I need to tell you, I began.

She looked at me, much as a higher form of life looks at the lower.

– Yes, she said. What is it?

– Well, we've been getting on, I like you a lot and I think you should know I've got cystic fibrosis.

– Oh, I know that, she said, without missing a beat.

– You do?

– Of course I do. You've had the drugs in your bathroom every night I've stayed here and since I can read labels and search the internet, it took me about five minutes to find out.

I shuffled uneasily in my seat.

– And you cough a lot, which is a bit of a clue really, she added.

Now, six years later, we sat before a GP, despite my warnings to Kathryn that it was a waste of time.

– Just give it a go, she said. I've done some research and things have moved on further than you think.

Again, she was right. Her GP referred us to a specialist at the Bristol Centre for Reproductive Medicine. If you've never had IVF, it's difficult to communicate how little mystery or sensuality is left in it by the time a consultant's finished explaining the mechanics of the process.

– It's called intracytoplasmic sperm injection, ICSI for short, he said as if that helped. I won't bore you with the details but when the problem of your infertility is to do with your sperm, this is the best answer we have. The basic difference between ICSI and standard IVF is that instead of lots of sperm and eggs doing their best to get it together, this is more of a one-on-one encounter.

– One-on-one encounter? I asked.

– Yes exactly. One sperm, one egg. It increases the odds.

I didn't understand how one sperm and one egg increased the odds of success but this type of problem-solving wasn't my speciality.

– But I can't, I said. I have cystic fibrosis.

– You *can*, Rob. That's the point I'm trying to make. Your tubes are blocked but the sperm, in most cases, is normal. It just can't get out. I believe we'll be able to extract the one healthy sperm we need.

– So I can . . .

I swallowed, unable to bring myself to say it.

– . . . have a child . . .

– Yes, that's right. You *can* have a child.

I felt a wave of emotion wash over me and I cried like a baby. Kathryn held my hand and when my eyes cleared I saw she was crying too. I guess the consultant had seen this many times and waited for decorum to return to the room.

– Right, he said, I'll get you on the waiting list for the procedure.

A few months later we began the treatment. I quickly learned that ICSI involved two jobs: an easy one and hard one. I had the easy one, a minor operation under local anaesthetic where they'd try and catch some good 'swimmers'. My balls hurt from the effort but other than that I was fine. Kathryn, on the other hand, was fed barrels of drugs, had her eggs collected and her embryos replaced. Then the waiting game began. The biology is clinically simple: our task was to make a blastocyst, an embryo made up of about 100 cells. A simple life form by any standards but my blocked tubes turned it into an act of creation of which the *Book of Genesis* would be proud. *And on the seventh day Rob rested*. Except I couldn't rest. Every day we waited for a progress report from the clinic. We needed the embryo to survive and keep dividing in the lab for a week before it could be transplanted back into Kathryn. I went into work as usual. For once, the distraction didn't work and I kept counting minutes, hours, passing the time imagining cells going from one to 100.

I can't remember what I was doing when I got the call. We'd made a blastocyst. In fact, we'd made several. Felling greedy, I asked if we could have twins. Theoretically yes, came the reply. However, it wasn't recommended. When you carry a disability or a chronic illness, recommendations tend to be emaciated, frugal things, one sugar not two, don't take your wheelchair on the motorway, marathons really aren't for people with bad lungs and twins . . . really? So I took Mum's perennial advice, ignored any thought of a limit and argued for twins until the consultant said twins were a risk to mother and babies.

The transfer of the blastocyst was a mechanical affair. After it was over, despite being a passenger, I craved a cigarette before remembering CF kicked that habit before it got started. We waited two weeks before Kathryn took a test and it was official: we were pregnant. (In common with most men, I use 'we' both as a signal of solidarity and a sneaky attempt to snatch the glory of pregnancy and the ordeal of labour without having to pay the price.)

Above all, I was disbelieving. I couldn't believe it worked first time. The consultant warned us against excessive excitement but he might as well have told a lottery winner to forget about the money. In the short interval between leaving the consultant and arriving back at the flat, we'd planned the colour of the baby's room, for both possible sexes, talked about where we'd go for our first family holiday and how I was going to design a new Trunki just for the baby. I named it 'The Improbable Trunki'.

In the days that followed I thought about the situation rationally: the odds of me being able to conceive a child had seemed so insurmountable, I reasoned the odds of getting from conception to birth had to be in our favour. The six-week scan showed our embryo was small but healthy and when we went in for the twelve-week scan I expected the same outcome. About two weeks before the scan, Kathryn said something didn't feel right. I told her not to worry. Everything was going to be fine.

I was wrong.

The scan confirmed we'd lost the baby. That's why *elpis*, hope or expectation, was the last of the evils in Pandora's jar, the one that wasn't set free, because it lends you a dream and lets you keep it until it's wriggled into every useless, hope-infested cranny of your psyche then, at peak happiness, it wakes you up. What can be worse than that?

Kathryn ended up in hospital and I felt what I can only describe as compound pain. I grieved for a life that was barely a life, my past grief rose from some dark pit where I'd kept it buried and I lost complete control. The baby, Kate's death, my terminal diagnosis, my mum's sadness, everything came at once. I'd made the mistake of allowing my life to be driven by inflated expectation. All my life, I'd done what I was good at, planned for the best, guarded against the worst, but kept myself anchored in the present. The thought of being a father shattered this habit. It hurled me into the future and when real time met my imaginary time, my dream collapsed.

I was totally unprepared for this loss. I remember watching a documentary about a prisoner on Death Row whose day of execution arrived. He ate his last meal and walked, calmly, to the execution chamber, only to be told the governor needed time to hear a last appeal. A few hours later the appeal failed and he returned to the execution chamber. This time he had to be dragged screaming to his death. He'd prepared for one course of events. When that course changed, he rediscovered hope and perhaps saw himself leaving the prison, eating with his family, being free. When that hope was taken away, he had no emotional answer. I'd lived a life resigned to never being a father. Then I'd been told it might happen. Then it did happen. Then it was taken away.

– We'll try again, Kathryn said.

– I don't know if . . .

I didn't finish the sentence. I just put hope back behind my wall with the CF. They were made for each other.

We did try again and three months later she was pregnant for a second time. This was easier on Kathryn as we used embryos we'd frozen. It was also easier because I refused to hope. I lived from day to day, working on the business, finding pleasure in knowing that Kathryn was carrying our baby. As for the future, I expected nothing. That expectation turned out to be prophetic. We went for the six-week scan. We held hands as we looked at the screen. We couldn't make out anything. The nurse fiddled with the image, making it bigger, changing perspective. Still nothing because there was nothing there. The womb was empty. There was no embryo and there would be no baby. I've heard many theories about the meaning of Nothing but there isn't a psychologist, mathematician, scientist or priest who can explain it with greater clarity of awfulness than the image on that screen.

I hated the capricious God who rolled the dice this way and that with no regard for the outcome of the game. I wouldn't let him win. *This time I lost, so I'll roll again.* Kathrine felt the same way.

– Let's keep trying, she said.

– Of course we will, I replied.

In life, as in business, we fail only because we give up too soon. That doesn't mean persistence is a guarantee of success. It can, and often does lead, to multiple failures. However, by driving on and picking yourself up every time you're knocked down, what you're doing is leveraging the odds in your favour and tempting luck to give you a break. There's a simple equation developed by the psychologists Daniel Kahneman and Amos Tversky, that says that success is talent plus luck and great success is talent plus lots of luck. And what is talent? To me, it's just another word for hard work. The more you do something, the better you get at it and the one thing that keeps us from trying is fear.

I've been scared many times: when I learned as a kid I had a terminal illness, when my sister died, when I watched, helpless as Mum was beside herself with grief, when Peter Jones called my product 'worthless', when four Dragons turned into a troop of chimpanzees, when Kathryn had our first miscarriage. But what I've never done is let fear dictate my actions. I stay focused on the problem at hand, reason my way to a solution, test that solution and review it depending on the outcome. It doesn't make me a better or worse person than anyone else. It just makes me who I am and gives me the ability to depersonalise any problem and detach it from fear or anxiety about the future. It also gives me the strength to value freedom over safety and to take calculated risks, most of which fail but one that succeeded created a new category of product and made Trunki into a global brand. Would my efforts to be a father give me the child I craved? I had no idea. All we could do was keep trying.

I returned from hospital, went straight back to work and made one of the most significant decisions I ever made in the history of Trunki. At first, everyone agreed with my decision then, a couple of years later, in the great rush to disown a disaster, everyone disagreed.

Harmony is always a good place to be, so I'll start with agreement. By October 2011, we'd manufactured a million Trunkis in China and organising worldwide distribution is fraught with complexity. Think of a supply chain as a chain that spreads out towards all corners of the globe and each link on the chain designates a point at which human or technological intervention is needed to move a product along the chain. Each of these points is both a mark of progress and a risk. Most of the risks are known risks such as the risk of a machine breaking down or logistical systems going offline. Other risks are more difficult to identify and some are unheard of until they happen. This last category would be what Donald Rumsfeld meant in his famous news briefing in the lead up to the second Iraq War where he said, 'there are also unknown unknowns – the ones we don't know we don't know . . . (and it is these) . . . that tend to be the difficult ones'. In supply chain logistics, they tend to be sudden, unforeseeable shocks to the chain that break it.

My solution to the management of these risks was to move a significant proportion of manufacturing from China to the UK. I don't think I'm ever certain of my motivations for the business decisions I make. What I am sure about is they're all attempts to solve a practical problem in the best way I can, using the best information I have to hand. The information is never more than partial, which makes my judgement subject to anything from mild to major error. I think of it like being on *MasterChef*, where you're given a set of ingredients and told to cook the best dish you can or being a jazz musician, where the most important rule is to improvise. People who struggle with that level of uncertainty should never attempt to run their own business.

So, back to my reasoning for manufacturing in the UK, specifically in Devon.

When I first started manufacturing Trunki, the pound was worth about two dollars, which made domestic production too expensive. That situation had changed and, by moving some of the manufacturing to the UK, I cut out one of the major risks, which was currency fluctuations.

The value of the pound relative to the dollar affected the unit price as well as shipping and fuel costs. This value can change quickly and, over three months at the end of 2008, sterling lost 25% of its value, which meant Trunkis were now 25% more expensive to produce. This made my margins unsustainable. I raised the price as high as I dared from £25 to £33 a unit. An extra layer of complexity was added to the process because the factories in China charged their costs in renminbi, which was strengthening against the dollar, leading to further cost increases at source.

The problems created by currency fluctuations were compounded by the inability of my real customers to forecast demand accurately. John Lewis rolled out Trunki in all their UK stores but significantly underestimated demand. I was now on a 120-day delivery schedule and supplies kept running out. There's nothing worse for a retail brand than being out of stock. It frustrates customers and leads to reputational damage. Winging it, I ordered in bigger bulk from China. While this helped to align supply and demand, it tied up cash in stock and warehousing. For any business, weakening cash flow is a mortal sin: it kills businesses. I made the problem worse by adding Tipu the Tiger, Bernard the Bee and Harley the Harlequin to the rapidly expanding Trunki family and, in an increasingly frantic attempt to resolve multiple problems, I ended up on endless flights to and from China. This had two negative effects: a further cash burden due to the repeat purchase of sacrificial underpants and an inability to communicate clearly with the Chinese manufacturers. They kept saying yes to my suggestions but it was done out of courtesy rather than understanding.

Perhaps the biggest problem, however, was that the reality of how Trunkis were made and distributed no longer reflected the values of the business. For me, values weren't a cosmetic addition to the Trunki brand; they were its essence and events were taking us further away from our core value of responsibility. While we were always

finding ways to improve levels of responsibility to our staff and customers, I felt our increased carbon footprint was an abdication of our
responsibility to the environment and I had to do something about it.

Restoring a UK production facility would solve this problem. It also
enabled me to redesign Trunki for the fifth time. Removing all metal
parts made the product 100% recyclable, quicker and easier to
assemble and safer for kids. Every part on a Trunki could now be
snap-fitted for easy assembly. Above all, having a production facility
in the UK allowed me to innovate in new ways and launch a Trunki
customisation service.

Decision made.

I set out the terms with Brian, the factory owner, in 2011 with a view
to starting production just before the Olympics in the summer of
2012. I had a clear vision of Trunki wearing Union Jacks rolling off a
British production line. Because my problem-solving skills are better
applied to product design and business than they are to people, I
didn't pay enough attention to a niggle I had about Brian. Entrepreneurs have niggles all the time. Usually they're worth paying attention to because most of our big decisions are made on the basis of
niggles rather than balance sheets.

If I were to be generous to myself I'd tell a *big lie* that goes like this:
I felt that Brian was a bit of a character but he'd been running this
factory for some time and knew much more about manufacturing
than I did, so I let him get on with it. If I wasn't being generous I'd
pick three mistakes in the *big lie*: first, if ever you hear yourself using
the phrase 'bit of a character' in relation to anyone, stop, say it again
and think very hard before you take them on and have any business
dealings with them; secondly, just because someone's been doing
something for some time doesn't mean they've been doing it well;
thirdly, if you're ignorant about any process that has a big impact on

your business, then learn quickly or find someone who isn't a 'bit of a character' to teach you.

So, what was the problem with Brian? It was obvious when I think about it now: it was the way he talked. A big, thick set man with a bulging stomach and ruddy complexion, he always greeted me with a smile. Generous and open in all his communication with me, I found him easy company and he came with a standard set of phrases:

– What will you have to drink, Rob?

– Great isn't it, Rob?

– We're going to set the world on fire, Rob.

These phrases washed over me but there was one that niggled. This was it:

– Don't worry about that. We'll figure it out.

Coming out of the mouth of someone whose judgement I trusted that phrase would be reassuring, showing as it does a willingness to battle through uncertainty. Every time Brian said it, I smiled as the niggle struck. Sometimes it showed up as a little twist in the gut, other times a sudden urge to scratch my face. The behaviour may have varied but the niggle was constant.

Then there was Mary, his wife. She attended most of our meetings and called herself chief administrator but when I asked her to specify what she did, the conversation ended with greater confusion than it began. She nodded when Brian brushed one problem aside after another.

– Can you cope with variations in the volumes we need?

– Don't worry about that. We'll figure it out.

– What if we need to increase production significantly at short notice?

– Don't worry about that. We'll figure it out.

– You've never manufactured a ride-on suitcase before or any mass production item: do you have the skills we need?

– Don't worry about that. We'll figure it out.

– You'll need to recruit more staff because Trunki will take 25% of your factory's capacity. Where are you going to get good people from?

– Don't worry about that. We'll figure it out.

So we cut a deal, shook hands and signed the contract.

There are always mitigating circumstances for every misjudgement. Mine was a visit to see the Queen. Shortly before agreeing everything with Brian, I went to Windsor Castle to collect my MBE. I still believed I didn't in any way deserve the award but I went to collect it with Kathryn and my parents. I saw it as a day for them rather than me. The logistics were pretty straightforward and explained to me at great length.

– You walk forward, then you bow, accept your honour, have a brief conversation with Her Majesty and make way for the next person.

And that's what I did.

I didn't feel nervous or honoured. I just felt humble and undeserving.

I noticed a man stood next to the Queen. When my name was called, he leant towards Her Majesty and whispered in her ear before beckoning me to step forward.

– Congratulations, Mr Law, the Queen said as she presented me with my MBE. I understand you make little suitcases for children.

– Yes Ma-am, I replied.

I can't remember anything else other than, in the moment she spoke to me, I thought of my sister Kate.

Merited or not, I'd received an honour from the Queen and I came to Windsor Castle with a marketing plan. I'd designed and built a special Trunki for the day. Tipu the Tiger had volunteered to be covered in light brown fur so he could look like a corgi. I wheeled him around the castle gardens waiting for the perfect photo opportunity to come. The gardens were full of tents and people, so I pulled myself away from the crowds and that's when I saw, a short distance away, the Queen's dog walker, three corgis beside her.

I pulled my Trunki towards them. When she noticed me, she smiled.

– It looks like we're all walking corgis, I said.

We had a brief conversation and I asked if she'd mind if I took a photograph.

– Of course you can, she said.

So I did and the following day we distributed it on social media and on the website. It was one of the most popular images I ever took of a Trunki. It was after meeting the Queen that, in an unconscious way, I must have become filled with a sense of invincibility, which I took into my initial meetings with Brian. I can't and won't use it as an excuse, just an explanation. So when he said, 'Don't worry about that. We'll figure it out', what I heard was 'Don't worry about that. *I'll* figure it out', the 'I' being me, and that was the mistake that led to the second decision I mentioned above, the decision that, two years after it was made, no-one agreed with.

At the time of the London Olympics, that decision was a few months away. In the heady summer of 2012, Trunki was at an all-time high. Sales were soaring, the brand was strong and global, work was fun, the business was getting stronger and I took the whole team to see Sir Chris Hoy win gold on the cycling track. For the first time, we made it into the Top 100 fastest growing UK companies in the Sunday Times Fast Track sponsored by Virgin. That, however, was topped by an invitation to a garden party hosted by Richard Branson. Every one of the 100 top companies was invited and I thanked him by making a special Virgin Galactic Trunki. We painted the body white to match the White Knight spaceship with a carbon fibre saddle, translucent blue horns to represent the earth and a Virgin Galactic logo on the side. I'd bottled my mission to give the Corgi Trunki as a gift to the Queen, which was lucky since I could have been shot for carrying an unapproved suitcase towards her. This time, however, there were no such problems. I picked my moment, presented the Trunki to Richard and took a selfie.

Jack, the Olympic Trunki adorned with the official 2012 London logo and a burnt orange and turquoise Union Jack, got official recognition from the London Olympic Committee. The business got unprecedented publicity. Every major news network in the UK came to the factory and The Mothership to film Jack and interview me about the business and bringing manufacturing back to the UK. The effect on sales was extraordinary.

– Don't worry about that. We'll figure it out, Brian said as the orders poured in and I asked how he was going to cope.

I got a call from him in November.

– Can you come to London for a meeting, Rob?

– Is everything alright?

– Nothing we can't figure out.

Before the meeting, I went to an awards dinner at the Hilton Hotel in Mayfair. We'd been nominated for SME of the Year at the National Business Awards. Trunki has won well over 100 awards ranging from Best Travel Product to Best Consumer Design, but this award was the only one I really wanted to win.

And we did.

When the envelope was opened and the host shouted Trunki, our table erupted. When I went on stage to collect the award, I thanked the entire Trunki team because it was their award as much as it was mine. That night I partied until dawn and when I got back to my room I coughed my guts up. Despite the searing pain on my chest I lay on my bed, hammered and happy. I slept like a baby.

A couple of weeks later I made the journey to the meeting with Brian. Despite my efforts, the MBE and SME of the Year award had taken its toll on my ego so I was due a reminder of Mike Tyson's wisdom, 'If you are not humble, life will visit humbleness upon you'.

That reminder came in the form of a simple statement:

– I can't figure this one out, Rob. I've run out of cash. The factory's going to be insolvent in a few days.

Life, like business, turns on small details. Like a knock on a door or a few, small words.

– Why didn't you let me know earlier?

– I wanted to but . . .

– . . . you thought you could figure it out.

– Sorry.

And that was how the best year in the history of Trunki ended. I didn't know it at the time but it was a prelude to a chain of events in 2013 that would turn my personal and professional life upside down. I'd have to rethink my business and my values and face the biggest fight of my life, where the survival of everything I'd built was at stake.

Cash and Copies

2012 ended with two sentences.

The first was mine:

– I'm going to buy the factory.

The second was Kathryn's:

– Let's try again for a baby.

Resurrecting a bust factory and sorting out my problematic personal plumbing felt like two sides of the same problem, both equally unsolvable.

Ever the optimist, I went to my local Footdown group, gave them my best pitch and waited for the seal of approval. Stuart, the serial shipping entrepreneur, was first to speak:

– Don't do it.

– But . . .

– . . . Just don't do it.

I looked around the room for support. A dozen or so faces looked back at me. All of them pursed their lips or shook their heads. A police chief looked at his shoes. They were clean.

I can't remember much about the rest of the discussion except that it sounded like a pathologist when the autopsy's done and he's spilling out a few gothic pleasantries to pass the time.

– Factories go bust for a reason, someone said as we left.

– I know, I replied, except I wasn't interested in reasons. My gut said *buy the factory* and when the gut speaks, the brain follows.

Entrepreneurs like talking about their gut. I do too. It makes us feel like we have some esoteric knowledge when all we're doing is turning our accumulated business experience, with its biases and ingrained habits, into a firm decision complete with justification. When faced with the self-evident truth of a business owner's gut, there are no spreadsheets or financial projections that are convincing enough to drive a change of course.

The reason for this intransigence is more straightforward than it seems. When our gut decides we're making a fast, unconscious decision, usually supported by a series of biased stories that run something like this: *The last time I trusted my gut, the end result was good so what should it be any different this time?*

There are four big problems with this statement.

First, your gut is biased and when you hear yourself say 'the last time', what you mean is 'the time I'm choosing to remember'. If a dispassionate observer who has no investment in your gut were to do an analysis of the times your gut decided, he or she wouldn't be as convinced of its wisdom as you are. Secondly, the real reason we trust our gut is because its workings are familiar to us. Psychologists call it an unconscious habit. I call it making the same mistake over and over again, then convincing ourselves we're right, even when our rational, analytical brain has evaluated the evidence and proven that we're wrong.

Thirdly, because our gut is emotionally driven, its conclusions *feel* compelling. That's not because the conclusions are right. It's because they're irrational and that gives them weight. In his famous book, *Moneyball: The Art of Winning an Unfair Game*, Michael Lewis told the story of how the Oakland Athletics baseball team used sabermetrics (baseball statistics) to build a team that was able to compete successfully against much richer rivals like the New York Yankees. Predictably, the general manager, Billy Beane, who introduced this statistical method, faced stiff opposition from his scouting staff, who believed their experience gave them better judgement than any mathematical analysis could ever provide. They were, predictably, wrong.

Finally, and this is the biggest problem, the biological cost of using our brains (measured in terms of consumption of oxygen, blood glucose and other metabolic resources) is too high. If we had to rationalise and analyse every decision we had to make, we'd never make any decisions at all. The alternative to being cast in this purgatory of indecision is to 'trust our gut'. Artificial General Intelligence may change this but for now we need to trust our gut. There are plenty of cases when your gut is right and I believed buying the factory was one of them. After all, experience must count for something more than the repetition of errors. Right?

This is how I rationalised my decision:

Having my own UK factory allowed me to innovate.

It helped leverage the Trunki brand against poor, badly made copies.

It championed UK manufacturing which I believed in and would lead to other companies approaching my manufacturing facility to make their products.

It secured British jobs.

I had Brian to run it for me, this time under my control.

Now, I fully accept that last point needed careful analysis but I chose to believe it anyway. So, 2013 began with me taking out a £500,000 loan, £40,000 of which was to buy the factory and the rest was to make it work. In business, when you trust your gut, it's also good advice to hire someone who's going to challenge your assumptions. I took on an accountant called Amanda. She had three key roles: to keep an eye on Brian, negotiate contracts and manage the factory.

When we began belated due diligence, we found that the basic building blocks of any business weren't in place. There weren't any HR processes and no-one had ever had an appraisal. At night, if the machines started producing scrap they should be shut down. They weren't, which meant they kept running, producing scrap from dusk until dawn. This was the Land of Headless Chickens and, as the man at the top of the pecking order, it was my job to reattach brains to bodies.

It didn't start well.

Tony, the technical director, resigned. His resignation speech went something like this:

– I hate him, Rob.

– Who?

– Brian.

– Why?

– Do I really need to tell you?

– Er . . . no . . . but . . . er . . . tell me anyway . . .

– Because he hasn't got a fucking clue what he's doing.

– Really?

– Yes, really.

Tony paused, waiting for me to say something. When I stayed silent he went on:

– Everyone else hates him too and his wife.

– Everyone hates Mary?

– Can you tell me what she does?

As soon as he said that, I realised I hadn't got an answer. Everything went blurry and the next thing I remember was Tony saying, '. . . and that's why I'm resigning'.

With Tony gone, Brian and Mary still in place and doubts swirling around my gut, I moved Brian from a leadership to a technical role and Mary became office manager. I should have moved them out of the business earlier but I believed I needed their knowledge, so I pushed the problem down the road. I also gave them job descriptions, which gave me an illusion of control. For additional ballast against a sinking ship, I promoted Amanda to general manager. Between us and Andy, my financial director, we refurbished the factory, built a canteen, bought some new equipment and led with the core value *Proud to be Manufacturing in the UK*. Things seemed to be picking up when, six months into her tenure, Amanda called me.

– Rob?

– Yes.

– Brian's time's up. He just can't do the job. You've got to fire him.

So I did. I got the paperwork in order, which included a settlement agreement. I played everything by the book. I couldn't afford not to. One of the great frustrations of running a business is having to be fair and reasonable to people who wreck your business. If the success of a brand is down to 'a thousand small gestures', then failure is down to the same gestures turned evil. The scariest horror movies, like *The Exorcist*, *The Amityville Horror* or *The Omen* are all about demonic possession, when good people turn bad. It's the same in business but the effects of the possession are measured in broken balance sheets rather than dead bodies. The cure in both cases is the same: exorcism. The difference in business is that you have to be nice to the demons.

– I'm sorry, Brian, I said after I told him.

An ashen-faced Mary had joined us for lunch. I've never liked firing people but the first rule of running a mid-market business is: *You can't afford to carry passengers*. The necessity of running a lean ship populated by capable people is essential in smaller businesses as the margin for error is less. In larger corporations, there's always somewhere for people to hide, which is why the level of commercial craziness is in direct proportion to the number of hiding places. At Trunki, and in thousands of similar businesses, there's no place to hide and nor should there be.

By now, I wasn't sure if things were getting better or worse in the factory. All I knew was I had to make it work. This wasn't because of the 'sunk cost fallacy' (the compulsion to multiply losses simply because you can't accept that your first loss really should be your last). Rather, it was because I knew I had to have a UK manufacturing facility. I may have chosen the wrong facility but since it was the only one I'd got and it was too costly to shut, I had no choice but to continue.

Despite these problems the business was doing well. Sales were growing. Trunki was still riding on the back of the success of the 2012 Olympics and confidence was high. Then, a few months before I fired Brian, I got an offer I couldn't refuse. That's not, of course, literally true. You can always refuse an offer, however good it is. In this case, I chose to accept it.

With the exception of a single investor who held a small stake in the business, I'd always protected my equity and I'd advise every entrepreneur to do the same, regardless of whether the business is growing or shrinking, strong or weak. Selling equity should only be done when the offer is above your minimum sell level (MSL): the last thing you surrender in business is control, even a little bit of control, unless you've got overwhelming reasons for doing so.

In this case, the offer far exceeded my MSL and the reasons for selling were overwhelming. The Business Growth Fund (BGF), the UK's largest investor in growing businesses, offered me £3.9 million for 35% of the business. Seven years earlier, four Dragons had offered me nothing and the fifth had offered me £100,000 for half of the business. Peter Jones said the business was 'worthless' and held little hope of his judgement being proved wrong. The BGF investment valued my business at £12 million.

It was a great deal for Trunki and a great deal for me personally. My original investor cashed out half his equity with £500,000, I pocketed £1 million net and the rest of the money, after lawyers had taken their share, was invested back into the business. It allowed me to open an office in the United States, invest substantially in product development and recruit a proven, heavyweight team to attempt, at the very least, to anchor my gut in reality and drive sales.

There was also another reason, the most important of them all, why I accepted the offer: Kathryn and I still wanted to defy the odds and start a family. The money enabled me to pay off the mortgage on a large apartment in Bristol with a garden, which was ideal for bringing up kids. It gave the family security if I should break my promise and let CF get the better of me. It also gave me a vision of a future where I wasn't working seven days a week, driving relentlessly forward, regardless of the cost to my health and the well-being of those around me. In my mid-30s, I'd reached a point in my life where I wanted a future that wasn't anchored solely to my business ambitions. I'd always baulked at the equation of childlessness with barrenness, especially in its broader social implications for women, but that's how it felt to me. Whenever I imagined a childless future, it looked like a vast desert stretching out before me. Compelled to think of myself and beyond myself at the same time, it was another lesson in humility.

Around the time I accepted the offer from the BGF, we'd already started IVF treatment for the third time. Despite the consultant's encouragement, I didn't feel like I was looking at the situation clearly. Quite the opposite in fact. If I put too much emotion into the situation I got lost in feelings of self-doubt and a sense of futility about the entire process. So I did what was best and saw it as a problem to be solved. I'd been told the odds of the IVF working for me were between 1-in-5 and 1-in-10, so I made a list of all the problems I'd solved with longer odds than that. It was a long list that began and ended with the fact that I was still alive. That made me feel in control of the situation without falling into the familiar trap of expecting success.

I'd listened to a podcast about the Stoic philosopher Seneca and his idea of the 'premeditation of evils', which means if you think about the worst outcome and then navigate ways in which you can survive it, it insulates you against most misfortunes. My gut liked that idea, so did my head and that's why, to this day, if I'm faced with difficulty I imagine the most negative outcome, find ways in which I'd deal with that outcome and start work from there. It's by far the most powerful self-help technique I've ever used and, unlike most of them, it works.

In relation to the IVF, the worst that could happen was repeated failure and the toll it took on Kathryn's emotions and her body. We agreed if that's what we had to put up with, then we knew we could deal with it. Like Mum always used to say, 'There's always people worse off than you, Rob'. In the age of 'safe spaces' and a 'culture of fear', stoical resolve can seem old-fashioned, as if it doesn't belong in the modern world. Yet I believe it's the attitude we need most. We're all stronger than we think we are. We can withstand adverse circumstances like suffering, illness and emotional turmoil, better than we think we can. If we're frightened of anything, it's usually our own strength. 'Our deepest fear,' wrote Marianne Williamson, 'is not that we are inadequate. Our deepest fear is that we are powerful beyond measure. It is our Light, not our Darkness, that most frightens us.' Because of Mum's attitude being drilled into me for as long as I can remember, I felt blessed to be alive and to have the possibility, however remote, of being a father.

Firing Brian also lifted a big weight off my life. When you carry indecision for too long and tolerate a situation you know you have to resolve, it becomes a drain on you personally and on your business. My problem was that I liked Brian and Mary. They were decent people trying their best to earn a living. and my awareness of the effect firing them would have on their lives, prevented me from doing what I knew I had to do. It's a dilemma every business owner has to face and the answer should always be to act quickly and decisively. Indecision doesn't solve the problem. It simply delays the inevitable and when you eventually act, more damage will have been done to your business. I remember seeing on the cover of an old leather writing pad, a quote from Shakespeare, I think it was from *Macbeth*, 'If it were done when 'tis done, then 'twere well it were done quickly'.

For any business owner and anyone deferring a decision, remember this advice. It will serve you well.

After Brian left, Tony, the technical director who'd resigned, re-joined the business. I also knew I had to hire an experienced production manager to restructure the manufacturing processes. It's always been my aim to fill gaps in my own knowledge by hiring the best available people. With James, my first employee, recruitment was easy because he was the only applicant. Now that Trunki was a global brand and attracting substantial investment, recruitment adverts attracted a large number of applicants. This role, however, was different. As a board of directors, we struggled to find production managers with the right level of experience. After an exhaustive search, it became clear that one candidate was significantly better than the rest and he also came recommended by the Manufacturing Advisory Service.

Doug had managed mass production facilities that were substantially bigger than ours.

– Thank you for giving me the opportunity, he said when I called him to make a verbal offer of the job. It's exactly the kind of challenge I'm looking for.

– Thank you for joining us, I said. You're exactly the kind of person I've been looking for, so we should make big leaps forward.

– I was wrong and so was Doug.

He'd been used to running operations that were already pretty smooth when he took them over. In any area of any business, taking over an efficient department or facility and improving it is much easier than trying to resurrect a failing factory run by a management team with little or no knowledge of direct factory management. Despite a promising start, the slow disintegration of Doug was as painful to watch as it was catastrophic for the factory. Amanda was closest to it and she gave me weekly then daily updates, all of which began with variations on a single statement:

– He's not coping, Rob.

Despite the reports turning gradually into what felt like bulletins from a war zone, I believed in Doug. From the moment I met him, he felt like a safe pair of hands. Every time he'd sort the mess out. He didn't. He left within six months. By the end, he had the look of a man who's witnessed unspeakable things and can't get them out of his head. His once amiable expression had become haunted. He said the right things but any belief he had in himself had vanished.

I've no doubt the pressures of turning a failing factory around took their toll on him but, speaking from what I've learned on my own personal journey through ill-health, it's the baggage you bring to the problem that makes it unmanageable, more than the problem itself. By trying to control what is not ours to control and through an inability to break a big problem into smaller, more manageable problems, we overwhelm ourselves. The fault, as the saying goes, is not in our stars but in us.

The catalyst for the dramatic transformation in the factory's fortunes turned out to be an obvious one that so many business owners often fail to see until it's too late: I assessed the talent I had on the factory floor, many of whom had been with the company for years, and decided to promote from within. First, however, I replaced Amanda, who'd only ever been an interim appointment, with Mark, a new general manager. Under his guidance, we pushed forward. He worked closely with Amanda during the handover period. New systems and processes were put in place and a new psychology swept the factory floor: positivity. Under Brian's oppressive regime, people turned in on themselves. Now they became an abundant resource of ideas and activity. Business and self-help books often miss how easy it is to effect change when you focus on the simple things. Most people in your life or your business have got something to contribute. Whether they do or not is down to the way you manage your relationship with them. 'Every yoked creature', the novelist George Eliot wrote, 'has its private opinions.' If you want to find what those opinions are, remove the yoke.

Over the next 18 months, the factory turned around. I launched *Made for Me*, a service that allowed kids to design their own Trunki. With 10 parts in nine colours there were more than a billion possible combinations for children to stamp their personality on their Trunki. Superheroes, pets, strange creatures, all rolled off the production line in a procession of children's dreams. I also estimate that eliminating 99% of freight from China has saved more than 100 tons of carbon, which is the equivalent of driving a car 200 times around the Earth.

As the bond with my customers grew stronger than ever, so did my bond with the team at the factory. I promoted people from the factory floor into management positions. By the time the factory became efficient and turned a profit, the £40,000 I'd paid for it had turned into a net cash investment of £1.7 million. Like all business lessons, it came at a cost but as long as you don't take losses personally and learn quickly, the pain is as necessary as it is valuable.

As for finding a 'bottom-up' solution to the problem as opposed to a 'top-down' solution, all I can say is that sometimes the answer we need is literally on our doorstep. We fail to see it because of a prejudice for doing things the 'right way'. When you've got a mess to sort out, it's always best to ask people who've lived in it to solve it rather than bringing in outside experts who may have a perfect CV full of the right kind of qualifications and the wrong kind of experience. Years later, after Mark had moved on, having solved many of our production problems, our new production manager was Ellie, a woman in her late 50s who'd worked on the factory floor for years. The talent's there – you just have to look in the right places and be prepared to take a risk.

As ever, running alongside the factory fiasco and its intimations of commercial mortality, my illness served me with regular reminders of my personal mortality. There were times when my lungs felt like they'd go the way of my factory before two weeks hooked up to an IV line brought me back from whatever dark cliff I'd been standing on. Then, in the spring of 2013, a miracle happened in my personal life. The scene of this miracle wasn't a stormy sea, the square of a great city or a lofty mountain peak. It was a small room with whitewashed walls covered in medical diagrams and the magic that made the miracle possible was science: Kathryn was pregnant for the third time.

At the time, it didn't feel like a miracle. We'd been here before. Twice. But there was a difference this time. We made it passed the six-week scan without a hitch. As I began to hope, Kathryn started bleeding on a train ride to Bordeaux during a holiday in France. We secured an appointment in a hospital. I don't remember what happened, only how I hated feeling out of control, teased with hope. The results came back. Everything was clear. The baby was doing well. Kathryn left the business on maternity leave and I presented her with a customised Trunki designed like Benny, our rescue cat she adored. We decided to offer it to John Lewis as an exclusive with a percentage of the proceeds going to the local cat rescue centre.

The pregnancy went full term and, in February 2014, a week after the due date, Kathryn did her best to relax in a birthing pool at the local NHS hospital, waiting for our first child to be born. The water was warm and reassuring. Carol, the midwife, was in there with us. Even this close to being a father, I still managed to keep my expectations in check. I'd promised myself not to hope until I held my baby in my arms and I was going to stick to my resolve. At just before five in the morning, the miracle happened and my daughter Ida was born, a very healthy 8lbs 5ozs.

I have no words to describe the strange, overwhelming beauty of seeing my daughter emerge into the water. A few minutes later Carol took Kathryn, who'd lost two litres of blood, for a check-up. I was alone with my daughter in my arms. She was more than I'd ever hoped for. It was my biggest triumph over CF and the proudest moment of my life. I cried as the baby in my arms slept.

When we got her home, I'd find myself watching her obsessively, partly out of love and partly out of fear that she might vanish, that my senses were deceiving me, that the whole thing was a cruel trick. I learned new things about CF. After years of living with the illness, it was only now that I discovered that sleeping babies and loud coughing don't mix. Determined to be a normal father, I shared responsibility for Ida's care with Kathryn. I ran my business, dealt with the factory, set up global distribution deals and drove myself with renewed energy now that I had a future that extended beyond my lifespan, however long or short that might prove to be.

Business success brought new demands on my time. There were dinners, social events, speaking engagements, endless meetings. In the six months after Ida was born, I worked intensely with my triathlon coach and I competed in two competitions. In the past, I'd competed in races and ran my business after a good night's sleep. Now I was doing it when my sleep patterns had become erratic.

– You need to sleep properly if you're going to do this, my coach said to me.

– I'll be fine. There's people worse off than me who do more than I'm doing.

167

– As long as you know the risks you're taking.

Of course, I knew the risks I was taking but they were different form the risks my coach thought I was taking. For him, the main risk was that I'd end up in hospital or die on the race track. I acknowledged and accepted that risk but for me the greater risk was not doing what I was doing. Every mile I ran, every metre I swam, every morning I got up at first light to care for Ida, every day I battled through the challenges the business gave me, was a day I was saying, *Fuck you CF*. The risk of not doing that was, for me, the greatest risk of all.

Suffering from exhaustion, I ended up in hospital for two weeks.

Before I was discharged, the doctor said to me,

– Life or death, it's your choice, Rob.

Three small words: life or death. Something had changed since Ida was born. I'd become a father and held my daughter in my arms. I carried the beauty of that with me every day of my life. But there was something else. Our lives, like our businesses, often change faster than we can adapt. We're always playing catch-up, trying to make sense of what's just happened and holding onto familiar patterns of behaviour in the belief the rules of the game are constant. But rules are never constant. What we value at one point in our lives may not be what we value at another. In the summer of 2013, I still didn't understand the depth of the change that being a father had wrought in me. For want of a better plan, I just kept on doing what I'd always done, with the addition of managing my new role as a parent. It was, predictably, too much and my lungs protested.

Lying on a hospital bed gave me time to reflect. I promised myself I'd take better care of myself but I'd never been good at that. I felt

CF was getting a grip of my body and my mind. I couldn't shake it off or persist in any form of denial. So, I committed to early nights, scaled back my business social life and, as a protest against these restrictions, committed to running two Half Ironmans.

Regardless of my willingness to change or my stubbornness in persisting with pushing myself beyond all reasonable limits, there was a big issue I had to deal with.

It began in February 2013 at the Nuremberg Toy Fair.

– There's a Trunki on a stand in the next hall.

Toby, the bringer of this news, was breathless as he spoke.

– What do you mean, there's a Trunki in the next hall?

– Just come with me.

We walked through a sweaty mass of people and made our way into Hall 2.

– There, he said, pointing at the PMS International stand a few yards away.

My first impression was how ugly it looked. While it was clearly a rip-off, it was badly painted with spots and stripes and none of the character or childlike appeal of a Trunki.

I approached the stand.

– What's this? I asked pointing at it.

– It's called the Kiddee Case, the rep from PMS International replied.

– It's an odd shape, I said.

– That's because children can pull it along using this strap here.

– Pull it along?

– Yes, like this.

He pulled the suitcase in a small arc around the stand.

– Does it do anything else?

– No, it's just a suitcase.

– Can I have look inside?

– Sure.

He let me open that case. It was badly built with cheap components. The catch was flimsy and almost came off in my hand. This was more than the Trunki sneezes: it was an aggressive strain of Trunki flu.

– Thank you, I said and left.

When we were back on the Trunki stand, I turned to Toby.

– They've copied the Trunki without understanding the product. It's too dull to be of interest to kids and too weak to carry them.

I don't know what irritated me the most: the fact they'd tried to copy Trunki or that they'd done it so badly. I'd already fought off more than 30 cheap copies from China but this was different: it was a British company and posed a bigger threat. I was ready for the fight.

My primary protection was the strength of the Trunki brand and my design registration.

The following day, the first battle of the Great Trunki War began when I returned to the stand with a letter.

– Hello again, the PMS International rep said.

I handed over the letter.

– This is from my lawyers. My name's Rob Law and I invented Trunki, the product you've tried to copy.

I waited for him to say something. He didn't. I went on:

– My lawyers insist you remove the product from your stand immediately.

– I'll have to talk to my boss, the rep said.

– If it's not gone within the hour, there'll be further action.

I retuned an hour later. The copy had been removed but I knew there were bigger battles to come.

A month after the toy fair, Toby called.

– They're still doing it.

– Who? What?

– I'm at the NEC in Birmingham and PMS International have that horrendous copy back on their stand.

I called my lawyers. They were familiar with PMS International and told me they were known for copying products. They reissued the letter I'd handed to them in Nuremberg. This time they told me they intended to sell 200,000 units in the next year and if I wanted to fight them, then bring it on. We followed up with a High Court application and an interim injunction based on an infringement of our design registration. We also attacked them for the copying of unregistered components like clasps and tow straps. They'd even copied, word for word, the safety notices that appeared on every Trunki. The Great Trunki War had escalated.

A date was set for a hearing at the High Court in London for July 2013. I'd just fired Brian, and Kathryn was recovering from her ordeal in a hospital in Bordeaux.

I asked my lawyer about the odds of a glorious victory. About 50%. I asked her what was going to be decisive in the battle. She was concise in her answer:

– Does the Kiddee Case create the same overall impression as a Trunki when seen from the point of view of the user?

– Of course it does, I replied.

– If only battles were that easy to predict.

There was no doubting the originality of what I'd created. Trunki was a new category of product. What the judge had to decide, was, if both products were manufactured in grey without any ornamentation or surface design, would a parent or a child be able to tell the difference? The case would hinge on the strength of my registered design rights.

Despite these warnings, I went into battle feeling confident that our case was strong. I'd designed Trunki and catalogued every element of the product. Beyond that, I had no control over the outcome so I refused to worry about it. A hearing was set for July at exactly the same time as I took the entire Trunki team to Barcelona to celebrate the BGF investment. I went for the first night and flew back to attend court.

I spent about an hour in the witness box being grilled by their barrister. I had an idea of how they'd attack. I was wrong. Their main line of attack was to claim that I could not have designed Trunki alone and therefore the design registration didn't belong to me.

– Tell me honestly, Mr Law, which components did you design yourself and which did you buy from other suppliers?

– I designed every component of Trunki from scratch. There's not a single piece of this product that I didn't design.

– Are you seriously asking us to believe you and all this work yourself without help?

Back and forth we went until the defence barrister consulted his client. Then he surrendered.

– Congratulations on designing a great product, Mr Law, but while we are not disputing your skill as a product designer we still claim that we have not infringed your design registration.

They accepted they'd given a Trunki to a Chinese bucket manufacturer and asked him to copy it. They said they were entitled to do it because I had no rights over the design. Their argument hinged on the fact that I'd disclosed the design publicly while still a student before I'd even thought of registering it.

The judge disagreed.

We won a crushing victory on all counts. The terms of surrender were made clear by the judge: PMS had to pay us costs, damages and a percentage of sales.

That should have been decisive except PMS International refused to surrender. They appealed. At the time, it didn't bother me at all. We won the first case, how could we lose the appeal? And that's when the Great Trunki War got dirty.

Courts and Losses

n sickness, death and business, the biggest lesson I've learned is that victory is never more than a hiatus in a series of defeats.

In a documentary about his life and work, Leonard Cohen said he 'found that things became a lot easier when I no longer expected to win'. Despite the obvious truth in this stoic view of the world, it's hard to let go of the illusion that a life of endless victories is worth chasing, but it's through our defeats, through not getting what we want, that we grow. In these moments, and every life has many of them, we learn what it is to be truly human and that is the greatest victory of all. I despair watching kids (and so-called grown-ups) fetishise fragments of a life on Instagram, Snapchat or Facebook and mistake the fragments for the whole. Real lives are messy and unpredictable and beautiful because of it. If we lose sight of that truth, we won't learn and we won't grow, individually or collectively.

I'd won the first battle in the Great Trunki War and if I was a Roman general riding my chariot through the streets of Rome in celebration of a glorious victory, I'd have a servant whispering in my ear: 'Memento Mori! Memento Mori! (Remember you shall die! Remember you shall die!)' In my case, I had my mum's voice in my ear, 'Count your blessings because you don't know anything about tomorrow.' That wasn't strictly true. I knew with absolute certainty that tomorrow would bring another problem to solve and then another and another. So, having won the first battle, I waited for the second.

It was between the end of the first battle and the beginning of the second that Kathryn safely carried our first child. When the date of the appeal was announced for February 2014, we knew the verdict would come within days of Ida being born. Despite this, my preparations for the appeal were as practical and rigorous as ever. Bundles of paper came and went. Meetings lingered longer than they should. Barristers gave upbeat predictions, which I didn't like. If there's one thing you want from a lawyer it's pessimism. That's what you pay them for, to be miserable, find holes in your defence, spot the cracks through which your defence will disappear.

A few days before the hearing, I made a list of everything that could go wrong in the next few weeks. Here it is:

My production manager might have a nervous breakdown.
The factory will descend into deeper chaos.
I won't be able to serve my customers.
The Trunki brand will be damaged.
I'll lose the appeal.
I'll lose my baby.

I carried each one of those eventualities to its gloomiest extreme and worked out in detail how I'd deal with each eventuality. The only one for which I had no answer was the death of my baby, so I got on with dealing with the problems I knew I could solve.

The appeal hearing went well. I didn't get to stand in the dock and face wave after wave of attacks by their barrister. This battle was more studious than the first with the outcome decided not by cross-examination but by legal interpretation. I found it easy to put proceedings out of my mind and get on with my life. The call came a few days after Ida was born. I was holding her when the phone rang. It was my lawyer.

– Sorry, I said, passing my daughter to Kathryn.

I walked out into the corridor. I noticed the insipid blue of the walls.

– We lost the appeal, she said.

– How?

– It's a long story . . .

After she'd finished, she concluded by saying,

– . . . at least if you're going to lose, you might as well lose a landmark case.

– First, I hate losing and, secondly, I don't care whether it's a landmark case or not.

The truth was I hated something more than losing and that was losing unjustly. Bleating on about justice or fairness is not, of course, a good place to be but I couldn't shake the feeling off. All my life I've treated people fairly, often too fairly. There have been many occasions when I've felt bewildered by disloyalty or the political machinations of office gossip and the wild rumours that spin off from it. I see little point in wasting energy on psychological fantasies and even less point in putting myself in the position of being a victim of circumstances over which I have no control.

This is easier to say than do. I knew from experience and, out of practical necessity, that I can't afford to be consumed by a sense of unfairness. Yet, for one of the few times in my life, the judgment of the Appeal Court left me seething with resentment. The depth to which I'd succumbed to being a victim can be seen in a few of the phrases I repeated to my legal team, friends and colleagues. I might begin with:

– There's no sense in this decision.

Followed by:

– How can they find against me on that evidence?

Then I'd sink deeper into the mire:

– It's so unfair.

And end with the worst phrase of them all:

– All that hard work and then this happens . . .

I knew in my head and my gut that this cycle of self-pity served no purpose other than to perpetuate itself at my expense but, when you're on the wheel, it's hard to stop spinning. It was the *reason* why I lost the case that caused me the most difficulty. It all came down to a line drawing.

I was a kid when I invented a new category of product called a ride-on suitcase. Because Trunki was unlike anything that had preceded it, there were no guidelines for me to follow on how to register the design. CAD was also in its infancy, so the representation of Trunki that I registered was a solid greyscale design. That was in 2003. Eleven years later, the Court of Appeal had decided that it should have been a black and white line drawing. The judge said that a solid greyscale representation of the product means that only a solid colour version of Trunki was protected and there was no protection for surface decoration.

If I'd submitted a black and white drawing in 2003 then I would have won the appeal because grey was deemed to protect any colour but not the surface decoration, while black and white was regarded as a representation of any colour *and* surface decoration. The problem was that in 2003 there were no guidelines to advise me on how to register Trunki and certainly no ideas on how a court might interpret that advice. To make matters worse, the judge concluded that

> . . . the overall impression created by the Trunki registered design is that of a horned animal. It is a sleek and stylised design and, from the side, has a generally symmetrical appearance with a significant cut away semicircle below the ridge. By contrast the design of the Kiddee Case is softer and more rounded and evocative of an insect with antennae or an animal with floppy ears. At both a general and a detailed level the Kiddee Case conveys a very different impression.'

After the verdict, to stop myself from wallowing in rage and self-pity, I called George, my PR adviser.

– This is big news, Rob.

– Can we make it bigger?

– Absolutely.

He was as good as his word. After the defeat, many of the world's leading designers expressed their support for Trunki and disquiet at the verdict. Sir Terence Conran, Kevin McCloud and Paul Smith were just three of those who feared for the future of innovation and design as a result of the Appeal Court judgment.

The case began to get national headlines. The *Daily Telegraph* ran a feature entitled 'Celebrity Designers Rally Round Trunki'. This time the Dragons were on my side and they were breathing fire. In an open letter to the government, Conran, McCloud and Smith were joined by other 'industry heavyweights' including Will Butler-Adams, the MD of Brompton Bikes, Shaun Pulfrey, the inventor of Tangle Teezers and Adam Balon, co-founder of Innocent Drinks. They said the ruling 'puts British businesses, compared to their European counterparts, at a real disadvantage. This lack of harmonisation and clarity is unacceptable for British designers and, we believe, of sufficient importance to warrant re-examination by a higher court'.

The support of friendly Dragons and hundreds of letters and emails from customers and members of the public that flooded into The Mothership gave me a timely reminder of the importance of humility. It also turned my inward-facing self-pity into an outward-facing battle cry. After such overwhelming support and positive publicity, I made a decision to take the case to the Supreme Court for a final judgment. I said to The *Daily Telegraph*: 'I urge the Supreme Court to re-examine this muddled judgment and do the right thing – not only for Trunki but for the hundreds of thousands of creative and innovative British companies that make the UK a thriving economy'.

I also took to the streets along with some members of the Trunki team. We carried pictures of Trunki and Kiddee Cases and asked random members of the public if they thought the pictures were showing the same product. Without exception, everyone said yes and a significant minority said, 'They're Trunkis aren't they?'

After they'd answered the question, I quoted the bit when the judge talked about the difference between 'an insect with antennae' or 'an animal with floppy ears' and 'a horned animal'. Responses varied between people looking at me like I was tripping or asking me if the judge had taken an illegal substance before making his decision. To compound the situation, families who'd bought Kiddee Cases were posting pictures on Facebook and Instagram, thinking they were Trunkis.

With the PR all going in my favour and the publicity driving sales, it felt like I was reliving Dragons' Den. Rejection in the Den and failure in the High Court both had the effect of increasing the visibility and desirability of the brand. On a personal level, it reminded me of the importance of never, ever, being a victim. In life and business, there's always adversity to deal with and injustice to combat. The best way to do it is to refuse to be a victim. I'm not saying this as a moral crusader but as a practical and successful entrepreneur who's also battled terminal illness: we only have so much time and energy, so we can't afford to waste any of it. When our resilience is tested, especially when it's tested publicly, the choice we have is to turn against ourselves or fight. There's no middle ground in this. If we turn against ourselves, we'll lose our business and much more besides. If we choose to fight, then it's vital to fight with a calm, rational focus, with what the philosopher Friedrich Nietzsche called the force of a hammer and the precision of a tuning fork.

The test of whether we're winning or not is what I call the '3 am challenge'. If you're waking up at three in the morning, with voices banging away in your head, running and rerunning the same self-defeating grievances over and over again, then you're losing. If you sleep well (allowing yourself only an occasional 3 am moment) then keep going. With that mindset, whatever the eventual outcome, you'll find a way to turn it to your advantage and if you don't adopt a winning mindset, you've only got yourself to blame.

Disappointingly, the two ways of managing adversity had a similar effect on my cystic fibrosis. If I turned against myself, I'd feel the pressure on my lungs building, my intake of medicines became erratic, the mucus poured out and I ended up having a brief stay in hospital. However, if I fought back, calmly and rationally, I tended to push myself beyond any reasonable limit, driven with a relentless determination to win, which meant I'd feel the pressure on my lungs building, my intake of medicines became erratic, the mucus poured out and I ended up having a brief stay in hospital. It seems, then, that the energy it takes to be victim and to refuse to be a victim had the same effect on my illness.

As ever, I thought the best antidote was to run. Triathlons, two Half Ironmans, all ended with me crossing the line, shouting, *Fuck you, CF!* before coughing my lungs all over the road.

In the summer of 2015, when Ida was 18 months old, I was preparing the case for the Supreme Court, Kathryn stroked what little hair I had left and said,

– I'd like another baby.

This wasn't a novel idea. We agreed that if we had one, we'd have another. I told myself I'd slow down this time. Even as the idea came into my head, I knew I was kidding myself.

– Nice to see you again, the consultant said when we returned to the clinic to begin treatment.

– I wish I could say the same, I replied.

They'd frozen my sperm from last time, so it was all down to Kathryn. I was a passenger and all I could do was support her on the journey. We took a break in South Africa and began treatment a week before the Supreme Court hearing in November. It worked. Kathryn got pregnant. After the success of Ida, it was hard to keep our expectations under wraps, but the court case helped.

The *Guardian* ran a feature titled "Trunki v Kiddee: battle over children's luggage reaches Supreme Court." They quoted a legal expert saying the case was 'likely to have profound implications in the design world, whichever way the Supreme Court rules'. I ran a #ProtectYourDesign

Twitter campaign, which began with a tweet saying, '350,000 design-ers contributing £16bn to the economy, yet copyists can get away with stealing designs'. George, my PR consultant, worked the online and offline media. The coverage was powerful and in my favour. I had to win this time. Surely?

However, even victories can be ruinous. The legal and commercial costs of the Great Trunki War was approaching £1 million. With no end in sight, I raised additional finance from shareholders. This was a difficult war to fight and there were few backers. The terms I was offered were extortionate, so I had a choice: concede defeat or take the deal. I took the deal. I've often been asked did I fight on out of vanity and the answer is no. I fought because I believed I'd win.

Any business owner, product buyer or serial seducer will tell you that first impressions count and, when I walked into the Supreme Court on the first day of my final appeal, five judges faced me. All male. I studied them one by one. I didn't get a good feeling. I went through the usual routine. Briefings in cramped meeting rooms. I didn't get to speak. I did, however, have a masterful battle plan. My lawyers had got a senior representative from the UK Intellectual Property Office to ask the judge to pass the case to the European Court of Justice on the grounds that the implications of the judgment were far-reaching for British and European designers.

Judgment Day, the final act in the Great Trunki War, came in March 2016.

Kathryn was five months' pregnant. The baby was doing well. The CF was behaving as well as could be expected in the circumstances. Trunki sales were booming. And remarkably, the factory was doing rather well, so all I needed was one more miracle. It didn't happen. I was at my desk at Trunki Towers about to leave on a flight to Hong Kong when the call came from my lawyer.

– We lost, she said.

The Supreme Court refused to defer to the ECJ and found in favour of Kiddee Case, the 'insect with antennae' and the 'animal with floppy ears', *not* the 'horned animal'. I felt numb. Then I got a plane to Hong Kong to get on with the rest of my life. This time there were to be no new court battles to fight. I'd lost the Great Trunki War. In one of the business groups of which I'm a part, the CEO of a pharmaceutical company once said: 'It's not the winning of the argument that counts. It's the sticking of the boot in afterwards.' PMS International didn't pass the opportunity to do so. They were awarded costs and damages.

The ruling was final so there was nothing I could do to change it. What I could do was turn it to my advantage. On the way to the airport after I'd been told the verdict of the Supreme Court, I called George, my PR guru.

– We lost, I said.

– Okay, he replied.

– How do we win?

– Leave it to me.

Within hours, he'd contacted his network of journalists and, as before, the tide of public opinion was in my favour. Sales went up in line with the publicity the ruling generated.

The case made global headlines. Every television network, more online platforms than I could name and every major UK newspaper covered the story.

Trunki had been on a long journey. It had fought Dragons, changed the way kids travelled in every continent on Earth and now it had lost a war. The BBC featured the story in the main news and the BBC website published a news article headed "Trunki loses ride-on animal suitcase court case." Before publishing the article, they called me for my reaction. I said I was 'devastated and bewildered by this judgment not just for ourselves but for the huge wave of uncertainty it brings to designers in Britain'. To rub salt in the wounds, the Supreme Court had cut into the work of British designers. I tweeted, 'this decision will create chaos and confusion among Britain's design community'.

The *Daily Telegraph* was more dramatic in the way it handled the story: *Trunki Inventor Rob Law says lost appeal was 'punch in the face' but it won't stop him*. It quoted Lord Neuberger, head of the Supreme Court, as saying it was with 'some regret' they had come to the decision. I wasn't interested in regret, mine or anyone else's. The decision was the decision and there was nothing I could do about it.

The Stoic writer Seneca wrote that people 'lose the day in expectation of the night, and the night in fear of the dawn'. A life bounded by fear of the future and regret about the past is not a life worth living. It's certainly not the mindset of successful entrepreneurs. It breaks resilience and saps our energy.

I told the *Daily Telegraph* that 'the ruling has created a lot of uncertainty. But there's nothing we can do now. We have to put it behind us'. I went on to say that 'we survived 2006, when hand luggage was banned for kids. We got through the Lehman crash and I haven't been discouraged yet'.

Despite my bullishness, the court case had taken its toll on my business and my health. My business was running at an operating loss. You only need to take your eye off your business for a short time and you risk losing what control you have over its future. Successful entre-preneurs live and breathe their businesses. If you want to switch off, don't ever think about running your own business. The margins for error are thin, the competition is fierce and your biggest competitor is yourself. 'Beating the competition is easy,' said Phil Knight founder of Nike, 'Beating yourself is a never-ending commitment.' While my experience of fighting PMS International suggested otherwise, Phil's right. My battle was and always will be with myself. A life in busi-ness means taking unfair and repeated blows. You can't control who strikes you or where the blows come from. What you can control is how you respond and that's the essence of what he's saying.

A common mistake entrepreneurs make is to fight battles they can't afford to fight and which they're likely to lose. They make things too personal. I've always lived by the principle that I'll only fight if I think not fighting will be more costly and I've got a reasonable chance of winning. That's why I took PMS International to court. It's easy to say in hindsight that I should have foreseen defeat but I didn't. When I took on the case I thought I'd win. Even after I lost the appeal, I thought I'd win. That wasn't misplaced optimism. It was a rational decision based on the legal advice I'd been given, victory in the first battle, backing from the IPO and my own beliefs about the strength of my case. It was a calculated risk and I've never been afraid of taking risks.

In our culture, the importance of risk in personal and commercial growth had been devalued. We're surrounded by experts who tell us that risk is bad and safety is good. If we continue down this path, we'll breed a generation of infantilised adults, unable to withstand criticism, who believe they have a right to be protected from harm and who blame anyone but themselves for the difficulties and challenges they face. We're bringing up a generation who no longer hesitate when harm is *probable*. Rather, they cower when harm is *possible*.

The very possibility that things might not work out as we want causes us to shelve projects and rail at the unfairness of the world.

The entrepreneurial mindset, on the other hand, doesn't fear uncertainty. It embraces it. The contrast between the fearfulness of the modern world and the healthy attitude to risk adopted by ancient cultures is summed up by the Roman senator and historian Tacitus, who wrote that 'the desire for safety stands against every great and noble enterprise'. Facing uncertainty is the only way we can grow. To shrink from the battle is to be less than we are capable of being.

What matters most when we go into battle is that we don't make it personal. In one of the most famous sports interviews ever conducted, Kevin Keegan, then manager of Newcastle United, threw the League title away because he allowed the necessary focus on footballing tactics and ability to get lost in a personal argument with his rival Sir Alex Ferguson. In a live interview on Sky TV after his side had lost, he blasted Sir Alex for what

> he said about Leeds, and when you do things like that about a man like Stuart Pearce, I've kept really quiet, but I'll tell you something, he went down in my estimation when he said that. We have not resorted to that, but I'll tell you, you can tell him now if you're watching it, we're still fighting for this title, and he's got to go to Middlesbrough and get something, and . . . and . . . I'll tell you, honestly, I will love it if we beat them. Love it.

Sir Alex went to Middlesborough. He won 3-0. Keegan lost momentum and saw the title disappear along with his composure.

That's what happens when you make battles personal. Of course, as every entrepreneur will tell you, battles can and do get intensely personal. Customers don't pay their bills on time. Competitors want to destroy you. People lie and cheat. The key to success is to deal with it, not moan about it and, if you've lost unfairly, accept it and move on.

However, despite my pragmatic approach to life and business, fighting PMS International took a lot out of me. On the trip to Hong Kong after the ruling of the Supreme Court, I had a terrible time with my physiotherapy and I was erratic in taking my medication. I stayed less than a week. I talked to manufacturers and distributors. They asked me about the case, more out of concern for themselves. In business, if anyone in your supply chain gets into trouble, check the effect it has on you: if it's not severe then offer sympathy; if the effect is very severe offers lots of sympathy and ask for a cash payment.

By the time I got home, I was exhausted. Trunki was all over the news and sales were at a record high. As I'd argued 10 years earlier when Theo popped the strap hook and Peter Jones mocked the absence of a patent, it's the brand that matters and Trunki is the original and the best ride-on suitcase available anywhere in the world. I'd been through so much in my life and I knew I could get through this. My optimism was given an unexpected boost when Bath University made me an Honorary Doctor of Engineering. I received the news with the familiar feeling that I didn't deserve the award. It did, however, give me the opportunity to talk to the students assembled in Bath Cathedral about the importance of passion and resilience.

But there was something gnawing at me. Ida was growing up. In April 2015, she'd ridden her first Trunki, which happened to be Benny the Cat, the one I'd made for Kathryn. We'd gone to my brother's wedding in Scotland. After landing, there was a long walk to baggage collection. I pulled her all the way. I tried to explain to her that Daddy invented the Trunki. She smiled as if that mattered to her then asked me to keep pulling: a journey I was never supposed to make with a child that could never be born on a product I was told was worthless. In sharing that moment with my own child, I learned the deep, heartfelt beauty of what it means to defy the odds in life and business.

When we got to the hotel, Kathryn was resting on the sofa.

– I don't know what I want anymore, I said.

She stared out of the window without replying.

– That's not like you, she said, turning towards me.

– I guess it's not, I said.

Over the next few weeks, the real financial hit to the business of the court case and my disjointed focus became clear. At the next board meeting, Andy, my financial director, who'd put credible growth strategies in places, took me through the spreadsheets.

– If you take the factory and the court case and the operational problems these combined events caused, then you're looking at a significant loss.

– How much?

– Look, he said, putting his numbers on the big screen.

He was right. They were significant.

– How can we get the numbers back to what they were? I asked.

– We need to cut costs and refocus the business.

– Then that's what we'll do, I said.

We acted quickly and some cuts to the team. I hated it. There's a mistaken belief that you have to be ruthless to succeed in business and I'm about as far from ruthless as you can get. I am, however, decisive and a realist. My core belief is that every business problem has a practical solution and the shadow of failure grows to the extent that we defer the difficult decisions we know we have to make, so I made the cuts.

As we shrunk the overhead of the business, I was about to double the size of my family. It felt like one part of my life was gradually taking over from another and, in August 2016, Kathryn gave birth to our son Rafe. There was no birthing pool this time. We'd arranged a C-section and, shortly after he was born, I held him in my arms, rocking gently, as I watched the men's triathlon at the Rio Olympics. Against all odds I was the father of a girl and a boy, both of whom were happy and healthy. I was still in my late 30s but that was older than middle age for a man who should have been dead in his teens.

I knew there was a decision looming. My drive to succeed in business was as strong as ever. This time, however, it had competition. I'd created a new category of product, sold over 4 million units in more than 100 countries, confounded the predictions of some of the world's leading entrepreneurs, survived against the odds and now I'd defied the longest odds of all: I'd become a father.

I've always said that my passion for design is driven by a capacity to solve practical problems and not allow myself to get diverted from that path. But that's not the whole story. I'm a big kid at heart and product design takes me back to that feeling of wonder I had as a child about the incredible way things worked. The fact that I could never be an astronaut didn't stop me dreaming of flying through space or walking on the surface of the moon. Every Lego spaceship I built filled me with wonder: What strange and beautiful planets will it fly me to? What creatures will I meet there? We lose that sense of wonder as we become adults. The world becomes too real and it breaks our imagination.

The reason Trunkis are based on characters, animals or spaceships with real names is because I've never stopped loving what it means to be a child, full of fun and curiosity. So, the next time you pull your kids on their Trunki along the departure lounge of an airport, take a moment to lose yourself in the world you may have forgotten about but which is as real to them as the plane they are about to board.

My adventure with Trunki took me to meet Dragons in Dens and a queen in posh rooms with high ceilings. I built a tower full of Trunkis. I called it The Mothership and every time a parent tells me how much their kids love Trunki, I always ask the kids to tell me about the adventures they've had with Terrance or Trixie or Tipu Tiger or Trunki-aurus. Their stories always surprise and captivate me.

Journeys in life and business should never lose the capacity to feed our imagination. And now I have my own children with whom and through whom I rediscover the roots of my creativity, I found an answer to one of the most important questions we ever ask our-selves: What is the meaning of success?

Toys and Toddlers

The months after Rafe was born were some of the most beautiful I've ever had. Ida was now two and a half and grew more confident and engaging by the day. Rafe just slept and poohed and cried and smiled and that was more than enough.

This time I took a more measured approach to my role as a father. Instead of driving myself to an inevitable hospitalisation, Kathryn made sure I balanced my roles as Trunki Daddy and Real Daddy without killing myself in the process.

Above all, being a father gave me a sense of what really mattered. Fighting the Great Trunki War and turning the factory around had cost me and the business a small fortune, yet despite the ongoing struggles at work, having children put everything in a clear perspective. It was as if all my problems were like layered coatings on a ball and, as each one fell away, they revealed a hidden truth and that truth is the meaning of success.

The biggest mistake we make is to imagine success as self-aggrandisement, a compulsive narcissism that feeds on outward displays of wealth and power. We're like the popes, kings and princes of the Middle Ages, competing to build the tallest cathedral. If asked, the great cathedral builders would say they were serving God. It's easy to say they were serving themselves but, in truth, they served neither God nor themselves because they were chasing the wrong dream. Success and the status that comes with it can never be found outside ourselves. They have to come from within. Yet we find it so difficult to understand this truth. Many entrepreneurs live by Malcom Forbes' famous maxim, 'He who owns most toys when he dies, wins'. So, the first question we must ask in life and business is, *What dream are we chasing?*

If we take Malcom Forbes' view, the dream is the acquisition of an endless array of 'toys'. When he died at the relatively young age of 70, he had acquired a private jet, superyachts, a vast art collection and was famous for hosting lavish parties. This *hunger for more* is, at least in part, biologically driven. The evolutionary psychologist Geoffrey Miller suggested that, in a Machiavellian struggle for reproductive success, 'our brains are different from those of other apes, not because extravagantly large brains helped us to survive or to raise offspring, but because such brains are simply better advertisements of how good our genes are'. The meaning of all our effort, then, is to chase 'toys' to prove our genetic fitness.

Fitness demands authenticity, which means the 'toys' must be the real deal. In the world of brands and conspicuous consumption, cheap copies may be indistinguishable from the real thing but it's the authenticity of our excesses that matters. The most copied brand in the world is Louis Vuitton. There are many online forums outlining how to separate an authentic Louis Vuitton product from a fake: handles wrapped in plastic or paper, a seam at the bottom of the bag, asymmetrical logos, the font, even something which can only be spotted under a magnifying such as the way the logo is carved into the zippers. Again, a consumer wishing to spot a real Louis Vuitton bag from a fake has to pay attention to detail because, as in all copies, the difference is visible if you look hard enough. However, while many fakes are very sophisticated making it extremely difficult to spot the difference except by close examination, you can't count them in Malcom Forbes' posthumous totting up of 'toys'.

So, after the birth of my second child, I looked at my business. I'd created a very fertile brand: Trunkis were now sold in over 100 countries and it was one of the most copied brands ever developed by an SME. Despite the problems with the factory and the loss of the court case, the business had enough strength to turn itself around and, over the next few years, that's what it would do. Like Steve Jobs and Jonathan Ive, I believe that 'innovation is what distinguishes a leader from a follower' and having children gave me new opportunities to innovate.

The Trunki brand is built around the needs of parents as well as children and every parent understands how taking a toddler to the shops can become a marathon as children explore an endlessly fascinating underworld of dead leaves and litter or dawdle on their bikes and scooters. My first attempt at solving this problem was to attach a Trunki tow strap, which converted into a shoulder strap. While this meant parents could also carry the bikes and scooters, they were at serious risk of an accidental homicide on passing pedestrians. The ideal solution was to develop a folding bike and scooter that could also hang on the back of a pushchair. There were two ways of doing this. One was to manufacture it ourselves. However, this would require high development costs, new factories and retail channels in addition to massive investment in inventory. The better way of doing this was to co-develop the products with Halfords, the largest retailer of bikes and scooters in the UK. This de-risked the project financially while leveraging the strength of the Trunki brand among children and parents. It was perfect for both businesses and it went on to be a great success. Innovation, then, isn't just about product design. It's also about business strategy and finding the best route to market.

If my children inspired me to innovate, they also changed my priorities.

I'd never chased material possessions. My great joy is to lose myself in solving a design problem, cut a deal that grows the global Trunki brand, run a triathlon and pushing myself to the limit. But now, blessed with two children, a very different future stretched out before me. It's a truism that many entrepreneurs, especially as they get into early middle age, change their perspective on success. They want to share their success, to give back to the wider community that has enabled them to be successful. That's not to say there aren't plenty of business people who ruthlessly chase 'toys' until the day they die but there are more ambivalent ideas of success advocated by some of the world's most successful entrepreneurs.

Many, perhaps all, of these entrepreneurs embody a Jekyll and Hyde approach to wealth and charity, none more so than Andrew Carnegie, the most contradictory of the nineteenth century "robber barons". Ruthless in his pursuit of wealth, he was equally driven to give it all away. He summed up the philanthropic impulse when he wrote that 'he who dies rich, dies disgraced.' By the time of his death in 1919, it is estimated that he had given away about US$350 million and he summarised his philosophy in what became known as the *Andrew Carnegie Dictum*: 'To spend the first third of one's life getting all the education one can. To spend the next third making all the money one can. To spend the last third giving it all away for worthwhile causes.'

Today, philanthropy is both more common and expected of entrepreneurs. Bill Gates set up a charitable foundation in 1994, just short of his 40th birthday. It is now the largest foundation of its sort in the world, with the aim of giving away the 'large majority' of his wealth during his lifetime. The Foundation is also committed to giving away all its money within 50 years of the death of Bill Gates and his wife Melinda. The main focus of the Foundation is on healthcare and alleviating poverty in developing countries and on increasing educational opportunity in the United States.

One of the key supporters and funders of Bill Gates' charitable work is the investor Warren Buffet, whose wealth is estimated to be second only to that of Gates himself. Buffet's attitude to wealth is similar to that of Carnegie and he has pledged to give away virtually all that he has to charitable causes. He described the disparities in wealth between rich and poor as an 'insult to an equitable world', and his determination that wealth should not be monopolised by successive generations of the same families has led him to leave his children sufficient in his will 'that they could feel they could do anything, but not so much that they would feel like doing nothing'. Together with Bill Gates and Mark Zuckerberg, the CEO of Facebook, he has committed to the 'Gates–Buffet Giving Pledge', which commits all signatories to give away at least half of their wealth to charity. Entrepreneurs are as inventive in their philanthropy as in their creativity. The publishing tycoon Felix Dennis made his fortune out of paper. In his early 50s, he began to plant a forest of indigenous, deciduous trees, which will grow to become the biggest forest of its kind in the UK.

Time and money give successful entrepreneurs time for reflection on mistakes they've made and the meaning of their success. Inevitably, this leads to a desire to contribute to the wider community of which they are a part. 'The world is too much with us,' wrote Wordsworth, 'Getting and spending . . . We have given our hearts away.'

And where was my heart? Few people have ever created a new category of product or marketed it successfully around the world while battling a terminal illness. But I never began the journey into business to feed my ego. I began the journey because I loved what I did and because I made a promise that my mother wouldn't suffer the loss of two children. I've also contributed to charity, both financially and with my time. I'm an ambassador for the Prince's Trust, where I raise awareness of the charity and use my story to help young entrepreneurs be resilient. It's easy to criticise entrepreneurs for the money we make, but it's a hard, relentless slog and without the entrepreneurial mindset our economy would collapse overnight.

I'm also patron for the 65 Roses Club, part of the Cystic Fibrosis Trust and I hope I can play my small part in finding a cure for this disease so no more children have to die like my sister Kate and many others who have lost their lives to this debilitating disease.

Above all, I love inspiring children with the idea that anything's possible. I've worked extensively with design and technology departments in schools throughout the UK, using Trunki as a case study to help them discover a passion for creativity. My interest in making education practical and entrepreneurial also extends into universities and I sit on the board of the University of the West of England who awarded me my second Honorary Doctorate. My role is to encourage students to become more enterprising and to give them the confidence to innovate.

By 2016, I'd also brought two children into the world, a daughter and a son for me, a granddaughter and a grandson for my parents. The psychologist Maslow claimed the highest of our needs is what he called self-actualisation. For me, that meant serving something greater than myself. We are all passing through life, some of us faster than others, and what matters is how we live our lives and the legacy we leave behind. That legacy isn't how much wealth we created, it's how much kindness we showed to ourselves and others. Being kind means, above all, refusing to judge ourselves and others for the mistakes we make. Perhaps the biggest mistake we make is to think success is a destination, a point we reach or the size of our bank balance or the 'toys' in our playroom. For me, success is simply living with humility and refusing to be a victim. It also means living a meaningful life and having children gave me a new purpose. Before my children were born, a friend told me:

– I hope you're ready for what's coming, Rob.
– What do you mean?

– Kids! They'll take your money and your time. They'll keep you awake at night and when they get older, they won't thank you for the sacrifices you made.

He was certainly right about keeping me awake. My efforts with Ida put me in hospital and, even with Rafe, I struggled balancing work with raising a family while avoiding long stays in hospital. What my friend didn't say was how readily I would give my life for my children. This wasn't anything rational. From the moment they were born, it was an inner knowing, a feeling so strong it's overwhelming.

In the winter of 2016, in the months after Rafe was born, I felt the balance of my life shifting. Trunki will always be important to me and I can't imagine a life without any involvement in business. The shift, however, was decisive. Faced with protecting the future of my children and spending what time I have left raising them with Kathryn, the decision to spend less time at work and more time with my children was an easy one to make. A lifetime of spending endless hours traveling or working late in the office, melted before Ida and Rafe. Every problem reduced in scale or disappeared completely before them.

I'd built a great team at Trunki with a passion for the brand. A key lesson I've learned is to let go when you see people doing your job as well as or better than you can do it yourself. That was now the case at Trunki and, with the business in safe hands, my first step into my new life was to reduce the hours I worked. Initially, I worked a four-day week and now it's a three-day week. This means my time at the office and promoting Trunki is even more precious because it's a legacy I'll leave to my children and success in business is what's given us the stability as a family to live the life we lead.

In the summer of 2019, about the time I began work on this book, Kathryn gave birth to our third child, a beautiful boy called Kip.

He was three weeks premature but in good health. He will be the last new member of our family. Despite the fact that I have just completed my first 6 km open water swim, I know my health is not getting any better. Yet, the children give me the strength to keep going, to keep fighting, to squeeze every last drop of life out of every day I have left.

As a parent, one of the most important gifts we can give our children is to be their witness. This means seeing them for who they are and loving them without judgement, even when we get frustrated by their behaviour or the demands they make on us. This, of course, begs the question we must all ask ourselves at some point in our lives: who will be *my* witness?

The answer for me is easy: the grandchildren I'm told I'll never see.

A Ride on a Trunki

When I recount the moment Theo popped the strap hook in Dragons' Den, I often say I wish I had a time machine that could take me back in time so I could make the strap hook strong enough to pass the 'Theo Test'.

Today, I'd rather have a machine to take me forward in time, so I'll end this book by taking an imaginary ride on a Trunki to meet my grandchildren. Please allow me this fictional journey, it's the most important one I'll ever make . . .

Before take-off, I look at all the Trunkis I've ever brought to life from Terrance and Trixie to Percy the Police Car and Pedro the Pirate Ship. I have affection for them all, but for the journey I'm about to take, I choose Skye the Spaceship. I love the idea that she glows in the dark as I imagine it must be very dark when you travel through time.

I make Skye a little bigger than a normal Trunki as she's going to carry a 43-year-old man. I also give her a few added features like a calendar to tell me what year I'm in, booster rockets and a key to start the engine I've attached to the bottom. When I've finished making her, I wait until the moon is full and the stars are shining brightly in the night sky. I pull Skye onto a launch pad I've built on the roof of the Mothership.

I turn the key.

The booster rockets fire and we have lift off!

I was wrong about the dark. As Skye races through time, light speeds towards me in thin beams until I feel surrounded by elongated stars and planets. Who said I'll never be an astronaut?

I look down at the dial . . . 2021 . . . 2025 . . . 2035 . . . 2042 . . . 2055 . . . and that's where Skye stops.

It's day. Morning. The sun shines across a green valley. I clamber off Skye and stretch my arms. The countryside is still and peaceful. I listen to my breathing. I can barely feel or hear it. I listen again. The same. I focus on my lungs. They're light. The familiar wrenching and crunching of the mucus isn't there. If it's 2055, I must be 78, although when I look at my hands my body hasn't aged.

Everything feels . . . *normal*.

I shout at the top of my voice and sprint across the dewy field. The green and blue of the landscape is crisp and beautiful. The faster I run, the freer I feel. I run until I slump against the trunk of an oak tree and close my eyes.

I hear voices. Children's voices, shouting, laughing, playing. I open my eyes. A boy and a girl running, another boy being pulled down the field on Skye the Spaceship.

The girl is the first to see me.

– Stop! she shouts.

The children stop pulling Skye and stare at me for a while. I guess the girl, who's wearing a coat and small, green wellington boots with animals painted on them, is about seven. The boy riding on Skye looks a little older, nine perhaps. He's holding what looks like a phone in his hand, although it's much smaller than any phone I've seen. The other boy, the only child with light hair, looks nervously across at me. He's wearing a T-shirt with a Superhero I don't recognise leaping across the front.

They hold their hands across their faces as the sun shines through the tree, directly into their eyes.

– I don't bite, I say as quietly as I can.

There's a long silence before the girl says,

– Were you the man who fell from the sky on this old Trunki?

– Yes I am and how do you know it's a Trunki? I ask, bewildered.

– Because our grandad invented them, the fair-haired boy says.

– And we know it's very old, the other boy says, because now Trunkis are everywhere and they talk to you and do errands and stuff..

– Just like the other robots we have, only better, the girl says.

– But I've never seen one fly like yours, so perhaps it's not very old . . . the fair-haired boy says, trying to make up for some imagined insult.

The children look nervous and I realise I'm just staring at them.

– Did you say . . . your grandad . . . invented the Trunki . . .?

– Yes, the dark-haired boy says. My grandad's name was Rob Law. I was named after him and Mum talks about him all the time.

– What's your mum's name, I ask?

– Ida, he says.

– And my dad's called Kip, the fair-haired boy says . . .

– And my dad's name is Rafe, the girl says. They're brothers and sister, she adds.

I keep staring at my grandchildren, absorbing the girl's blue eyes, the ferocity I see in the dark-haired boy's stance and the fair-haired boy, twiddling his fingers nervously.

– What are *your* names? I ask.

– I'm Robert, the dark-haired boy says.

– William.

– And I'm Kate.

– Of course you are, I say, smiling at her and before any of the children speak, I ask Kate,

– Where's your grandfather now? Does he live nearby?

The children hesitate before Robert says,

– He died, a long time ago, before we were born.

– We only know about him from pictures and videos . . . William says.

– And Trunki, Kate says. But our parents talk about him a lot.

– What do they say?

– Well, Kate went on before the boys could jump in. They say he took two Trunkis into a den full of dragons and he got beaten very badly but he never gave up and did incredible things like run triathlons and meet the Queen and he made so many Trunkis they were ridden by children everywhere . . .

– Come closer and look at me, I say and the children race forward. I turn to face them and that's when they recognise me.

– Grandad! Kate yells, before stepping back. You look just like in the old photographs. . .But . . .

By this time I'm pretty sure I must be dead, otherwise I'd be coughing my guts up and mucus would be spilling onto the grass.

I open my arms wide. Kate and William run into them. Only Robert holds back. He's checking the device in his hand. He looks down at the screen then at me before repeating the sequence until he, too, runs towards me.

I cry as I hold my grandchildren but I don't know what I feel. A voice from the past yells at me,

– Just tell me what you feel, Rob.

– I can't . . . I just can't . . .

And perhaps I don't want to.

– Is that it, Rob? The voice says, harassing me.

– Yes, it is.

The firmness of my response dissipates the voice and brings me back to the present and my morning under the oak tree with Kate, William and Robert. As if to vindicate my own mind, the questions they ask are practical:

> How you get here, Grandad?
> How can a very old Trunki fly through time?
> Did you really meet the Queen?
> And slay Dragons?
> How many triathlons did you run?
> What's that in miles?

Then Kate hesitates, looks at me and asks:

– What happened to you, Grandad?

– I don't know . . . Then why don't you take us back? Then we'd know what happened.

– I don't think we'll all fit on Skye, I say.

– Of course we will. You made it bigger for time travel, so if we squash up, there's room for us all.

– But first, Robert interrupted, we've got to get in back up the hill, so then we've got a runway of sorts.

The children dragged Skye back up. It felt wonderful to run alongside them without feeling a mountain of mucus moving on my lungs.

– This looks good, I say when we get to the top. All aboard!

Kate sits in the front, followed by William, then Robert, with me at the back.

— Someone's got to push, Kate says.

The children look at me.

— That'll be me then.

I jump off and start pushing. Skye races down the hill and I'm just able to get on as the boosters ignite and she takes to the air. We rise up into the clouds.

— Turn the dial, I shout.

— Which way? Kate shouts back.

— Anti-clockwise!

I watch her turn the dial. The sun burns brightly then turns into night and shards of starlight shoot past us.

Children's cries and laughter fill the night as Skye twists one way then another before she descends back through the clouds.

— Why are we slowing down? I shout.

— I don't know, Kate replies. Skye did it all by herself.

I recognise the scene below.

A cemetery. A man and a woman kneeling next to two graves. My mother and father. One grave has a large headstone. It's my sister's grave. Mum's laying roses across both graves. The grave on the left is fresh and the roses stand in vases that stretch the length of the raised earth.

Skye lands a short distance away in a corner of the cemetery.

– Can they see us? Kate asks.

– I don't know, I reply.

Mum looks tired. There's no headstone on the new grave but a long stick stretches out of the ground with a black plaque and some writing. *Robert Law. Died 21 January 2026. Age 49.*

I watch as they make their way out of the cemetery and pass within a few feet of us. They can't see us.

– Don't leave us! Kate shouts.

I'm sure they hesitate for a moment before walking on.

I'm numb, trying not to burst into tears.

– I made your great grandma a promise, I said.

– What did you promise? Kate asks.

I want to tell her but I can't. Watching Mum walking away, it's too painful.

– It doesn't matter now but I'll make you a promise instead.

– What? Robert asks.

– I promise I'll be there when every one of you is born. I promise you I'll live.

– Well, William says, if you make a promise you should keep it.

Before I can reply, the children begin to twist into strange shapes until they're gone and I'm alone on the roof of The Mothership, looking up at the stars.

* * *

If you make a promise you should keep it.

Given there are so few things under our control, how do we keep promises to live when faced with an illness timed to kill us in youth or middle age? Bernie Siegel, a former cancer surgeon, started a movement in the United States that spread throughout the world, when he noticed some patients defied their prognosis while others succumbed to it. He called those people exceptional cancer patients. Personally, I don't like that term. It suggests a judgement on those who succumbed. However, there is ample evidence that attitude and personal psychology has a bearing on whether we succeed at most things, from running a business to defying the prognosis of an illness.

So, if I died, how did I die?

I don't want to know whether I died coughing my guts on the bedsheets or collapsed running a triathlon. What I want to know is if I gave up, if I broke my promise and stopped fighting. That would be inexcusable.

I find it hard to read *Misery Memoirs*, where the protagonist struggles against the odds and dies at the end of the book. I hate feeling sorry for that person because I never want anyone to feel sorry for me. I've never asked for pity and I don't want pity. It's the most corrosive of all the emotions, especially when it mutates into self-pity. Of course, in the end, even the healthiest people die. What matters is how hard and how long we fight. I've seen businesses fail because the owners underestimated the effort they'd need to put in to launch their prod-uct or service and I've seen people die because they underestimate their ability to fight an illness.

While there are many ways to fight these battles, the conclusion I've come to is it's best to stay anchored in the present. Focus on those problems you can solve in the here and now because leaping into the future risks muddying your thinking.

From the moment I helped my father make things and listened to my mother telling me there's people worse off than myself and Kate, I've been grateful for every day of my life. Of course, that doesn't mean there aren't bad days. There have been plenty of them and there'll be plenty more. People will let me down, I'll make mistakes and let them down in turn and sometimes I'll lack the will to carry on. But through all this, I know as long as I keep myself anchored in the present and focused on problems I have a chance of solving, I'll defy whatever odds are put before me.

**

It's a crisp winter morning and I'm cycling to The Mothership.

When I get here, a few members of the team are standing outside, waiting for me.

– Are you alright? I ask.

– I think so, Laura, our Crew Commander, replies. It's just . . .

– Just what?

– You'd better come and see for yourself.

I get off my bike and follow Laura into The Mothership.

Inside, there are roses everywhere, blue, white, red, yellow, lilac. The scent is overwhelming.

– I counted them, she says.

– Don't tell me, there's 65.

– How did you know that?

She reaches down and hands me a note from the table:

You promised! Kate.

I stare at the note. She's right. I did promise and I'm going to make a pledge at the end of this book that you can hold me to:

Whatever the odds and whatever obstacles I have to overcome, I'm going to keep the promise I made to my grandchildren.

I know I can do it.

You can too.

AUTHOR'S NOTES

Thank you for coming on my journey and please let me know what you think of the book by writing a brief online review.

If you'd like to join me on my adventure through life, follow @trunkidaddy on Instagram and Twitter, find me on LinkedIn or check out #65rosesandatrunki.

You can find out about the latest adventures of Terrance, Trixie, Skye the Spaceship and the rest of the Trunki family by following #Trunki @ trunkitravels on Instagram & Facebook and @trunki on Twitter.

Should you wish to book me for a speaking engagement or deliver a keynote at a conference, please visit roblaw.com or email speaking@ roblaw.com

Once again, thank you for reading my book and my best wishes to you in life and business.

Rob.

ACKNOWLEDGMENTS

I am who I am because of everyone, good and bad, who have been a part of my life. Since I've only got one page I'll thank the good influences:

To Mum and Dad, who gave me the best start in life. Through constant encouragement, they enabled me to find my Element. Dad also helped out in the early days with the Trunki bookkeeping and creating our exhibition stands. More recently, he scoured the family photo archives for this book. Thank you Mum for always being there, ensuring I stay healthy and supporting me through the highs and lows of my journey.

To the CF teams at hospitals in Chester, Liverpool, Newcastle, Melbourne and Bristol for providing the support and treatment to keep me going.

To the anonymous donor of Kate's new heart and lungs that gave her a new lease of life and to Great Ormond Street for caring for her.

To Kathryn, for your steadfast support and for giving me the space to write this book. Thanks to Ida, Rafe and Kip for putting my challenges into perspective and for being my new driving force.

To all the teachers and lectures who helped me develop as a designer, especially Mr Davis who saw my potential at school and nurtured it. To my design peers, who inspired my creativity.

To Philip for being my first business mentor, and the Prince's Trust for giving me my first break. To Anne, for helping me see the bigger picture in life and not letting me avoid hard truths, and to my Footdown friends and the Campfire Collective for helping me navigate many business challenges.

To the Dragons for breathing fire – I may have got burned but the ordeal taught me valuable lessons.

To all my friends and teammates both past and present who helped make Trunki the global brand it is today, with special thanks to Trevor, my 'intergalactic ambassador', for his wisdom and guidance.

To George, who helped me kick off this project, and to Stephine, who helped secure a publisher and introduced me to Peter who helped write this book. Peter, thanks for helping me reflect on my challenges and achievements, for helping me journey safely back to the past and for crafting the story you have just read. And thanks to the team at Wiley for believing in the book and for your constant support.

To everyone who read the various drafts and gave invaluable feedback, to Phil whose creativity you see on the sleeve and to all those who kindly provided an endorsement for the book.

And finally, I'd like to thank the millions of children who take their Trunkis all over the world and who help me believe, even in my darkest moments, that anything's possible.

Happy Travels!

PICTURE ACKNOWLEDGMENTS

All pictures are from Rob Law's private collection with the exception of

Page 5, top, Western Daily Press
Page 7 Jim Johnson
Page 9 PA Images
Page 15, top, University of the West of England

INDEX